Whole Foods for
Babies & Toddlers

Whole Foods for Babies & Toddlers

MARGARET KENDA

la leche league international
Schaumburg, Illinois

First Edition, August 2001
First printing—8,000 copies
Second printing—2,000 copies
© 2001 La Leche League International

All rights reserved
Printed in the United States of America
Edited by Judy Torgus and Katherine Solan

Book and cover design by Digital Concepts, LLC
Cover photos and Part Opener photos by Subhadra Tidball

ISBN-10: 0-912500-85-9
ISBN-13: 978-0-912500-85-0
Library of Congress Card Number 2001091623

La Leche League International
957 N. Plum Grove Road
Schaumburg, Illinois 60173 USA
www.llli.org

In Memoriam—
Mary Margaret and Ryan, gone in the same breath and very much missed.

Contents

Foreword

Margaret Kenda's book will be extremely helpful to mothers who have infants and toddlers to feed. It gives the kind of information not easily found elsewhere. It offers an honest review of commercial baby food, informing us of just what is contained in those jars so expertly advertised as good nutrition for babies. Kenda also supports and confirms LLLI's recommendation to mothers that human milk is far and away the superior food for infants. She urges mothers not to deviate from giving babies the very best when baby is ready for solids. She urges mothers to make their own baby food from the same whole, fresh food used to feed the rest of the family.

Baby food companies do an excellent job of convincing parents that their product is highly nutritious. And mothers are not likely to give up the convenience of jar food easily. This book includes thought provoking information about the baby food industry and the huge profits that are generated.

LLLI cautions mothers to read labels before buying packaged or canned food of any kind. If the product contains certain undesirable ingredients we suggest you not buy it. In the case of baby food, however, reading labels will not help—it will only mislead. For example, in a jar labeled BANANAS, only 50 percent of its contents is likely to be bananas, the rest will be a filler, like tapioca. The rest of the family gets 100 percent fruit. Why deny baby the same? No mother would knowingly deprive her baby just for convenience; she has no idea that the food in the jar is not all it claims to be. Margaret Kenda has done the research for us and passes along the valuable information she has found.

Consistent with the need of the baby food companies to seek a good profit as one of their primary goals, each jar contains a large percentage of fillers. They know that such fillers are considerably cheaper than whole foods—veggies, meat, fruit, etc. These ingredients may be listed on the label but they are usually under names unrecognizable by the average reader. Then because the companies need to ensure that no bacteria or spores are left in the food, it must be cooked at high temperatures which further lessens the nutritional value of the jar's contents.

And if all of that isn't enough to make mothers want to create their own baby foods, there are those "hidden, unintended harms" to contend with. "Make no mistake," says Margaret. "Our children are targets. They are no longer protected from the most manipulative trends of modern marketing."

All of the above information found in this book was brand new information to me. I expect it will be to most who read it. It truly is in the best interest of the good health of babies and toddlers for parents to read what Margaret Kenda has to say about creating your own baby food versus resorting to convenient jar food which is low in nutrition and much more expensive. And you will not be left wondering about how to do so. She takes you through step by step as you begin, gives many good tips, and offers a number of great recipes.

We cannot be other than deeply grateful to the author for enlightening us in the matter of commercial baby food and helping us to choose the alternative—creating our own baby food—and thus joining us in our efforts to give babies and toddlers the very best food on the market!

This book is written by a mother who cares and you can't help but enjoy it. And it truly is in the best interests of your little ones to do so.

Edwina Froehlich
LLLI Co-Founder
May 2001

Introduction

Would you buy yourself a can of the lowest quality soup you can find? Then would you eat it directly out of the can, at room temperature? That's exactly how you could be feeding your baby—if you follow all the latest ideas on commercial baby food.

You can pay too much for convenience.

The commercial baby food companies are selling you convenience, first and foremost. They're trying to convince you that you're too busy to prepare food. You can't even be expected to mash a bit of banana with a fork. The latest sales pitch is to serve food at room temperature. Don't spend a minute heating up food for your baby. You're just too busy, and your convenience is everything, more important to you than good nutrition or a sensible approach to feeding your baby. Of course, your baby won't know the difference. A baby doesn't have any choice in the matter anyway.

There's no doubt about it. Commercial baby food is convenient. But there's one thing you need to remember. Convenience can mean that you're neglecting the health and well-being of your baby. You could be settling for poor nutrition at the absolute worst time, just when your baby is growing rapidly and developing what you hope will be a strong body and a powerful brain.

Convenience now can also mean you're giving your baby the wrong food message, a message that can last a lifetime. You're training the baby's taste buds to think that something like room-temperature, low-quality commercial food is what food is all about. You're teaching your baby to go for the minimum. You're falling for a sales pitch instead of making your own smart choices.

The commercial baby food ads are almost hypnotic. The companies sell you on mystique. They try to scare you just a bit about the idea of making your own baby food. They want to convince you that a jar of mashed bananas or a sugar-filled toddler dessert is somehow safer or cleaner or more valuable than your own simple, delicious homemade foods.

Don't pay more and get less.

Of course, their food is more valuable in one way. It costs lots more than home-made. A can marked for babies also, in most cases, costs lots more than other types of canned goods. The companies know you're willing to spend extra for your baby, and they try to convince you that extra money means extra food value.

The advertisers want you to believe that you owe your baby and toddler these designer jars, even at a premium price. The marketing makes commercial baby food sound almost like a prescription medicine, critical to your baby's survival. Without question, you would pay a high price to obtain a life-saving medicine for your child. Commercial baby foods, whatever the advertising, are just not in the same category.

Don't feed your baby a sales pitch in a jar.

This is a book on how to prepare and serve your baby real food, the best sort of nourishment for each age of growth. It's about real food, not bottles and jars of super-processed stuff marketed as if it were medicine. This is a book based on scientific research and an ongoing three decades of study into what commercial baby foods have to offer. Focused on the best ways and strategies to feed your baby, this unique cookbook could prevent you from falling for the latest food marketing schemes. It shows you straightforward, simple, easy ways to prepare the best foods for your baby. This book helps you avoid the dangers and cut the risks that surround modern food distribution. This book helps you deal with your own unique growing baby, whether your baby is fussy or mild-mannered, difficult or sweet-tempered, beset with physical difficulties or perfectly normal. You can use this book to help rescue your baby from the obesity epidemic. You can use this book to avoid allergies for your baby or to feed a vegetarian family.

Our recipes have been thoroughly tested. The classic *Natural Baby Food Cookbook* which I co-authored with Phyllis Williams was a book that parents trusted so completely over the years that the book reached its silver anniversary still in use. The recipes and ideas for WHOLE FOODS FOR BABIES AND TODDLERS are new, though, based on the latest food trends, cooking methods, nutritional research, and creative thinking. Real mothers and fathers prepare this whole food. Real babies eat—and thrive on—this food. Take control of your baby's nourishment and well-being. This book will help.

Part One

Issues, Obstacles & Goals

Chapter One
The Baby Food Industry and How It Tries to Trick You and Cheat Your Baby

Picture a bright, beautiful, little boy, much beloved by his parents. On the kitchen table are foods for this active child: a jar of precooked and processed spaghetti dinner and a jar of strained bananas. Inside the refrigerator is high-quality sliced turkey, and on the kitchen counter is a bunch of fine, fresh bananas. There are superior whole foods available for the rest of the family, but not for the baby.

But, of course, that's not how it looks to the parents. They do not deliberately give their precious child inferior foods. They are sold on the idea of good nutrition—from a jar. They don't realize that they can't trust those nice-looking, widely advertised jars.

Know the truth about commercial baby food.

The history of commercial baby food companies is, in general, not good. Their past would lead you to believe that you ought not to trust them for the future. All for-profit companies might be expected to work only for profit, but usually within ethical boundaries. In the past, commercial baby food companies have, all too often, shown they were willing to step over those ethical boundaries.

The most extreme example is from the 1980s when two Beech-Nut officials went to jail. They were convicted of selling apple juice that contained no apple. The "Beech-Nut 100% apple juice" was sugar water. The no-apple apple juice was a case of deliberate and conscious fraud.

But of course, the baby food companies can also fall into unintended trouble. There are the usual problems that go along with any industrialized food production. For example, in 1999, Heinz had to recall its Level Three "Broccoli, Carrots, and Cheese." People were finding shards of plastic in the jars.

3

The truth is that baby food is a global enterprise, turning over millions of dollars and millions of products every day. Like other modern corporations, their main dedication seems to be buying and selling other large (and medium) businesses.

Just try to figure out who owns what. Gerber is the number one producer of baby food, with a market share of 73 percent, and more than $226 million annual sales in the United States alone. Gerber is owned by Novartis AG. That's today. You may hear a different story tomorrow.

Maybe you prefer a smaller baby food company such as Beech-Nut. Beech-Nut is only number two (or sometimes number three) in the baby food market, with just over a 13 percent share. But even then, your baby food dollar staggers under the weight of making a profit for Beech-Nut—and also for its owner Milnot Holdings Company and also for Milnot's owner, an investment banking firm by the name of Madison Dearborn Partners, Inc

Or perhaps you are considering baby food from H. J. Heinz, usually number two or three, with under a 13 percent market share. Your dollar spent with Heinz is supporting a plan to take over Beech-Nut with a current bid of $185 million. A takeover like that would put nearly all the production of food for babies in the control of just two giant companies. The US government does not like the idea and in the year 2000 took Heinz to court to stop the purchase. So far, the courts have been deciding in favor of the government.

The market is just too concentrated on one big corporation (Gerber), with two backup producers (Heinz and Beech-Nut). It's a situation almost guaranteed to go against the best interests of consumers. Historically, in a situation like this, consumers pay more, and they get less.

So maybe you like the idea of one of the last remaining small, independent "gourmet" baby food companies, Earth's Best. But, wait, Heinz already bought them out. Earth's Best is just another name for Heinz now and Natural is just another name for Beech-Nut—until the next corporate buyer comes along.

Begin with bad food and graduate to worse.

Since commercial baby food companies are in business to make a profit, they want to sell more jars of food. Therefore, they typically seek to expand their markets downward to younger infants and upward to older children.

You may believe anyone is joking who talks about starting Gerber's cereal and bananas on the delivery table, until you read of a doctor who actually advises that babies start solids in the first hours of life. Talk about being in a rush to grow up! Now Gerber has outdone even that joke by marketing Gerber Mom, a milk additive designed to provide pregnant women with extra vitamins and folic acid—and also, not so incidentally, to make sure she satisfies her sweet tooth with a few extra empty calories.

Marketing upwards, the commercial companies sell to parents of toddlers, pre-schoolers, and school-age children—and then to children themselves. All the commercial baby food companies market something like Level Two and Level

Three foods for toddlers. If you want to keep your child away from fresh foods a few months longer, you could buy Gerber "Graduates" and Beech-Nut's "Table Time" in hyper-convenient, microwaveable tubs.

If you follow current food trends, a child might theoretically never eat family food. School-age children, perhaps the same children accustomed to those microwaveable tubs for toddlers, can go right on to microwave their own highly salted and frozen kid dinners.

All food could be play food. All tastes could be salt and sugar and starch—nothing real, tasty, or nourishing.

You need to know what's in your baby's food—and you cannot depend on a label to tell you. Look at even simple labels on a jar of baby food. For instance, you can find labels that say something like "BANANAS" and then underneath "tapioca." The type size gives you the impression, naturally, that the jar is full of banana, with just a bit of tapioca. Yet in a recent analysis, Gerber's best-selling banana food contains only about 50 percent actual bananas, with Heinz coming in at only about 30 percent bananas.

To figure out the more complicated labels, you practically need a law degree, an undergraduate major in nutrition, and a ready application of advanced statistical analysis. Even then, you can't tell the percentages. Percentages are not listed, although there are petitions before the Federal Food and Drug Administration to require them. Right now, you need to guess the percentages of the good, the medium, and the bad. Labels don't tell you whether there's a preponderance of bananas or the filler tapioca, of chicken or the cheaper noodles, of vegetables or chemically modified starch. But you can figure out one main point. You don't really know what is in those commercial jars.

By the way, don't necessarily believe every authority you hear, either. For example, some organizations with respectable-sounding names publish "Nutrition Fact Sheets" that defend commercial baby foods, along with taking other oddly unscientific positions. Behind the scenes, these may actually be funded by the giant food corporations themselves. If you'd like to learn more about how the commercial baby food companies operate, consult the Center for Science in the Public Interest at www.cspinet.org or see the CSPI book, *Cheating Babies: Nutritional Quality and the Cost of Commercial Baby Food* (Stallone and Jacobson 1995).

Watch out for cheap fillers and inferior ingredients.

Whenever there is an era of especially loud protest, the companies do drop some of their inferior ingredients. Then, as soon as the deafening roar subsides, they sneak the junk right back in again.

They're looking at the economic bottom line. Fillers such as starches (including flour and tapioca), sugar, and water are a lot cheaper than vegetables, fruits, and meats. The starches mask the addition of a great deal of water and replace the superior ingredients listed in the big type on the front of the label.

But keep looking. Even without spending an hour with a magnifying glass and a calculator, you can see even more objectionable ingredients in baby food jars.

Especially, look at the foods for older babies and toddlers. You may not like what you see.

Here are a few examples:

- **Not just one but a multitude of filler starches.** Look for thickening agents such as rice, rice flour, wheat flour, modified starch, chemically modified cornstarch, or tapioca. These starches are there to prevent ingredients from separating and thereby looking unpleasant. Starches also thicken the water and make the food look more substantial than it is.

- **Flavor enhancers** that go by a variety of complicated names such as hydrolyzed vegetable protein, autolyzed (or torula) yeast, caseinate. Flavor enhancers are often masking inferior or insubstantial food— and you can generally recognize them just by the vocabulary. They go by names you've never heard of.

- **Sweeteners** don't always go by the simple name of sugar. You might as well avoid baby food desserts altogether. Nutritionally, they're the worst of all the wide varieties of commercial baby food.

  Sugar Disguised with Many Names

Sucrose	Glucose
Molasses	Maltose
Cane Sugar	Malted Barley
Corn Syrup	Honey
Dextrose	Brown Sugar or Brown Sugar Syrup
Fructose	Turbinado

- **Salt.** You will rarely find salt as an ingredient any more, certainly not in the giant proportions that it's used in food for older children and adults. But be careful. The older the baby the food is intended for, the more chance there is that salt has been added—and not just a sprinkle either.

Commercial baby foods also present problems you cannot expect to find on labels. It is probably overcooked. The usual method is to get rid of bacteria and spores by cooking and cooking again. The bacteria and spores are destroyed, one hopes, but so is a great deal of nutritional value.

Compare fresh food with the jarred equivalent and you find that the nutritional value of the jarred food is only between 50 percent and 30 percent. Most of the value isn't there in the first place since it's replaced with inferior foods, water, and fillers. The rest hardly stands a chance with all that overcooking.

Don't be tricked, either, by a label listing nutrients such as iron, for example, as separate ingredients. The processing tends to remove much of the original nutrients. Then an artificial nutrient or two is processed right back in. These nutrients are all too often in a form that the body does not assimilate well or use completely.

Watch out for hidden, unintended harm in commercial baby foods.

Years ago, we were concerned about pesticides in baby food. Now, almost all baby food products contain just traces of pesticides. These traces are below federal standards. That's the good news. The bad news is that these standards are judging pesticide risk to the average adult. One can presume that pesticides and other poisons in food are harder on small children than on adults. But the federal standards—and the baby food companies—do not account for the huge difference between babies and full-grown adults. The standards ought to be much higher for children and even higher for babies.

This is a complicated problem, since, in the modern world, babies can be exposed to toxins from a multitude of sources. Even fresh fruit, drinking water, or milk can contain some pesticides. And there is no way to know the total effect. But at least we ought to be able to ask the commercial baby food companies to go beyond pointing at government paperwork. Insofar as they even intend to be responsible corporate citizens, they ought to be expected to use sensible and reasonable standards about pesticides—and to recognize the harm they can do.

Pay less and get more with your own baby food.

A jar labeled as baby food costs far more per ounce than food in similar cans and jars. Often, you can't make a direct comparison. But when you can, you find prices double or occasionally even triple any commercial equivalent. Baby fruit juices and varieties of applesauce, for example, unfailingly cost more than double the price of similar juices and applesauce marketed to the general consumer. Even the most expensive fresh food—including fresh fruits and vegetables—costs less than the overpriced baby food.

Essentially, when you put in time making your own baby food, you are getting paid and getting paid well. In the first year of a baby's life, North American parents spend an average of $500 on commercial baby food. That calculation includes parents who never spend a dime on commercial food because they make their own. So many parents must be spending much more than $300 on commercial baby food. There's no doubt they believe they are doing absolutely the right thing.

If you make your own baby food, you know for sure what's in it. You take control. Here are a few of the advantages, far beyond saving money:

- A lower percentage of preservatives.
- A lower percentage of risky ingredients such as sugar.
- Virtually no salt.
- No unnecessary ingredients such as starches and fillers.
- Natural nutrients generally in forms that the body more readily assimilates than isolated, artificial ingredients.
- Lower chance of ingredients that can cause allergies.

The baby food you create yourself is stunningly superior. Besides huge advantages in nutrition, you can give your baby other advantages with your own baby food. You create the texture ideally suited to just what your baby needs at each stage of development. As baby learns to handle, chew, and swallow food expertly, your food is ready at just the right level. Even better, you can shape your baby's tastes and preferences. Your child will know how fresh foods taste. Your growing child will naturally prefer the best, most nutritious food. The commercial companies will not be targeting one more easy mark. You will have given your daughter or son a lifetime advantage.

References

Stallone, Dorothy D. and Michael F. Jacobson. *Cheating Babies: Nutritional Quality and the Cost of Commercial Baby Food.* Washington, DC: Center for Science in the Public Interest, 1995. www.cspinet.org

For latest developments on the Federal Trade Commission case against Heinz, see www.ftc.gov

Chapter Two
The New Baby Food Problems— and How to Combat Them

The problems of a past era of baby food were relatively simple. You could solve most problems by making your own baby food. And you could join protests about the problems with commercial baby food. Both of these options are still, of course, excellent ideas. But now things have become more complicated.

Here are ten predictions that just about anyone could make about the future of our children's food. These, like all good predictions, are based on what one can clearly see in the present. Look around and you already see these scary trends happening around you.

We already live with the consequences of years of fat-engendering, nutrient-deficit eating. Unfortunately, we have every reason to believe this trend is accelerating.

As they grow up, our babies are liable to grow fatter than ever, at younger ages than ever. The obesity trend accelerates year after year, pound by pound (Piscatella 1997). Some nutritionists also claim that our food is causing children to suffer more mental disorders than ever, at younger ages than ever. Children, they say, are depressed. They're anxious. They suffer from attention deficit disorders. They have trouble learning (Simontacci 2000).

The commercialization of food will go mad with greed, if it hasn't already.

But the commercial companies that process our food aren't having any trouble learning. They've learned sophisticated new marketing techniques. They have developed innovative, cutting-edge ways to manipulate our emotions. They are experts at building magic, mystique, and mystery around what are just ordinary commercial products.

Make no mistake: Our children are prime targets. They are no longer protected from the most manipulative trends of modern marketing.

> *"For all practical purposes, the American diet is determined by market forces, not health concerns" (Jacobson 2001).*

The manufacture and marketing of food will become more and more centralized, even near the point of monopoly.

Already, only twenty corporations control nearly three-quarters of all food advertising. Among those targeting children are McDonald's, with its annual marketing budget of $1.1 billion. Almost all American children eat at McDonald's regularly, nearly 90 percent. And Coca Cola's annual budget to sell to us is $866 million. The food industry over all is spending $33 billion a year to reach you and your children (Schlosser 2001).

> *"The whole experience of buying fast food has become so routine, so thoroughly unexceptional and mundane, that it is now taken for granted.... It has become a social custom as American as a small, rectangular, hand-held, frozen, and reheated apple pie" (Schlosser 2001).*

The food industry will continue to reach our children at school.

Now even your friends may seem like enemies. In the last few years, schools are allowing vending machines stocked with soft drinks and junk snacks. The decision-makers say they need the extra money to promote educational programs, maybe even nutritional programs. Certainly, the vending machine decision does make a clear direct statement to children about food choices. It's education. It's just that it's harmful education.

And the harmful education can be direct, too. More than 12,000 schools in the United States subscribe to Channel One (and its competitors) with daily, televised, educational programming—and its commercials for junk food, fast food, highly processed foods, and soft drinks. Many pediatricians and other activists object to the required viewing.

We will live in a world of play food.

The choices of the commercial companies are always in front of us, so that we can get the impression that we have no choices of our own. Our children, especially, are in the grip of Happy Meals, Count Chocula, Gerber Graduates, microwave-ready tubs, Kid Cuisine (from Banquet), and Looney Tunes (from Tyson). There's always a new product, from deli meats with stamped-on smiley faces to the new child-attractive green ketchup. Of course, these fun, new, convenient foods tend to be expensive. They are hardly ever good for children (or adults either). They tend toward high fat, high salt, high sugar, and low nutrient value. (The strange secret is that these foods don't taste particularly good—unless you've become used to them.)

> *"Don't just stand there! Eat something!"–Bus stop advertisements for granola bars*

Families will continue to stagger along under pressure.

Parents will be looking for whatever help and support they can find, and commercial help and support will be increasingly available—for a price.

In more and more families today, both parents tend to be working outside the home at demanding jobs, often with long commutes and extended work hours. Many single parents don't have a spouse or partner to help. Even more have no extended family available locally. That's the inescapable sociology of the modern world. Of course, many families are finding good compromises and solutions to problems. They're taking control of their lives and the lives of their children.

But all parents must be tempted by products that save time and labor. More and more commercial goods will always be available. We can expect that, in the future, most foods will be sold as factory food, heavily processed, fully prepared, frozen, plastic-wrapped, ready for the microwave. For good or evil, future food will bear little resemblance to its origins on the farm or in the garden.

> *"At the risk of raising the guilt level of exhausted parents,…we hardly realize how removed we and our children have become from something as fundamental as food. Farmer Brown has been replaced by Ronald McDonald as the basic icon of eating…. If we are what we eat, we're oblivious"* (Goodman 2001).

More and more, children will eat alone, eat snacks instead of meals, and even prepare their own food.

Like adults, children often eat while doing something else, such as playing or watching television. Sometimes, children eat while running around, not exactly a physically safe activity. What they're not doing, all too often, is eating with their parents, at the same time as their parents.

The national trend is to replace regular, sit-down meals with snacks, often without the companionship of other people. Many older babies and toddlers unwittingly begin following the national trends as, day after day, they consume a continuous parade of snacks, one after another. Of course, these children don't want a regular, sit-down meal even when one is offered. They're not hungry then. They're never normally hungry and looking forward to a meal, because they've always just had a snack, are having a snack, or are about to have a snack. More than half of school-age youngsters—and their preschool siblings—expect to prepare their own convenience foods on a regular basis.

We live in an increasingly unnatural world, and we eat increasingly unnatural food.

For the first time, humanity stands on the brink of a life-altering agricultural revolution.

Scientists are learning to modify food crops genetically. That could be good. Genetic engineering can increase yield, helping to keep the world's six billion population from starving. Genetic engineering can mean crops will be more resistant to pests, drought, disease, and poor soil. It could increase the nutritional value of our food.

At the same time, environmentalists fear that the genetic revolution has a dark side. It is, after all, an unnatural intrusion into the basic foods that have provided sustenance for all human beings for all of eternity. We don't want to end up with unnatural, deformed "Frankenfood."

Or think of the other changes to the basic nature of food. We tend to eat fish from the calm and controlled waters of fish farms rather than from the overfished waters of the natural fish population. Are "designer" fish a good environmental alternative? Or are they liable to alter forever the genetic nature of a whole species?

At this point, the best we can hope for is to enter these changes thoughtfully. We need a healthy skepticism as we listen to each side. The future of our children depends on what happens next.

Our children's food will be increasingly complicated with vitamin additives and medicinal supplements.

Adults already tend to consume a variety of vitamin and semi-medicinal supplements. More and more, these supplements are blended into our food so that we are not necessarily even aware that we are ingesting them.

Among the many medicinal ingredients in ordinary food are an increasing amount of antibiotics. These are not the antibiotics that can knock out an infection and save your life. Instead, these are antibiotics hidden in food such as beef, chicken, and milk. An entire flock of chickens or an entire herd of cattle may be treated with antibiotics to treat infections. (You can't just identify and remove one sick chicken in a factory-style farm of thousands, and treat that one chicken. They are so crowded together as to be all exposed at once, and they must be treated all at once.) Or on another level, antibiotics are also used to promote growth in farm animals.

Yet as we (and the animals) take in more and more antibiotics, the microbes that they affect mutate and change. They're altering themselves to resist the antibiotics.

"People will believe almost anything, particularly if it sounds medical."
—*Julia Child*

You will be aggressively protected from knowledge.

This is one mega-trend that may be more easily resisted than others. There are always experts, paid off by commercial interests, who will tell you that the worst food is just fine. You don't need to be careful with food choices for yourself and your children. You can trust commercial forces to put your health first. You don't need to worry. Just stay happy and ignorant, no matter what you are seeing in your children.

Faced with these trends of the future, the best we can do is take control of our own lives and the lives of our children. We don't have to live out the expectations that the outside world foists upon us. We can stay ourselves and, to the best of our ability, defend our children from what the outside world wants of them.

References

Goodman, Ellen. If we are what we eat, we're in trouble. *New York Times* February 11, 2001.

Jaconson, Michael F. *Nutrition Action Health Letter.* Washington, DC: Center for Science in the Public Interest, January/February, 2001. www.cspinet.org

Piscatella, Joseph C. *Fat-Proof Your Child.* New York, New York: Workman, 1997.

Schlosser, Eric. *Fast Food Nation: The Dark Side of the All-American Meal.* Boston, Massachusetts: Houghton Mifflin, 2001.

Simontacchi, Carol. *The Crazy-Makers: How the Food Industry Is Destroying Our Brains and Harming Our Children.* New York, New York: Tarcher/Putnam, 2000.

For more about Channel One programming in the schools, see www.commercialalert.org

Chapter Three
Your Once-in-a-Lifetime Opportunity

The world urges you to hurry, hurry, hurry. You're supposed to be always in a rush, with no time to contemplate the world—or your baby. But babies are the ones truly in a hurry. They're doubling in size, tripling in brain power, developing lives of their own. You have a very short amount of time to influence their eating habits. You have only the years of very early childhood. Those are the crucial years, and what you do during them can make all the difference later.

> "Parents, in the first three years of your child's life, you have a window of opportunity to instill lifelong eating patterns. The food you serve and the habits you promote become your child's nutritional norms" (Sears and Sears 1999).

Babies develop the habit of eating convenience foods from a jar. They can all too easily grow up believing that fast food is acceptable, if that's all they've ever known. (It may not be McDonald's, but commercial baby food certainly advertises self as fast, convenient food.) Babies can reach school age believing that food is land sugar and starch, nothing more.

In the modern world, babies are born as the future targets of food marketing. They are subject to sophisticated, powerful manipulation, aimed at them almost om the start. In the first three or four years of your child's life, though, you are he one presenting what is normal for food. You are in control, and you ought to e in control of what your child sees as food. You're the role model.

If the family is choosing less than optimal nutrition, then the baby will be earning to choose less than optimal nutrition. And this will be happening at a uch younger age than you may want to believe. Picture your seven-month-old

15

baby reaching over to snatch food from your plate. Snatching food may not be good manners, but your baby doesn't know that. Your baby is just interested and curious. This is natural behavior, and whether you use special baby foods or not, this is how the future will be. Your baby will be eating as you do.

How do you act as role model? You eat well yourself. If you're eating vegetables and fruits, then you are that much closer to guaranteeing that your child is eating vegetables and fruits. You resist the eating-out, junk-food trends. If you're cooking good food at home, your child is eating good food at home.

"We make sacrifices every day for our children, and eating vegetables should be something we're prepared to do" (Pescatore 1998).

Given the rather common situation of a parent wanting to break the bad habits that a child has fallen into, it's easy to discover that bad habits are almost impossible to break. Too often, the parent is motivated. The child isn't. On the other hand, good habits are also hard to break. A child growing up with good habits, for the most part, will stick with good habits.

Being a role model is not easy, of course, especially since it requires you to be something of a nonconformist. Of course, your child will end up experimenting with mainstream ideas of eating. Your child will gorge cake and candy at a friend's birthday party. Your child will go on a school tour that takes everyone to a fast food restaurant. Your child will look around at the world and see (and try out) the 2000-calorie hamburgers, the mega-bags of French fries, the super-sized soft drinks, pizzas running over with grease, gooey snack cakes, and all the other nutritional (and taste) horrors of modern times. Your child will know it's all there and all too available. But your child will be the one who knows that's not all there is to food.

References

Pescatore, Fred. *Feed Your Kids Well: How to Help Your Child Lose Weight and Get Healthy.* New York, New York: Wiley, 1998.

Sears, William and Martha Sears. *The Family Nutrition Book: Everything You Need to Know about Feeding Your Children—From Birth to Adolescence.* Boston, Massachusetts: Little Brown, 1999.

Chapter Four
The Obesity Epidemic and How to Rescue Your Baby

The statistics are frightful. About half the adults in America are overweight. More than a quarter of the children are overweight. The government figures show that more than six million children in the United States are fat enough to endanger their health. They are suffering from illnesses once thought to be mostly adult problems: diabetes, heart disease, high blood pressure, liver problems, sleep apnea.

If we had any other problem that was this widespread, we would call it an epidemic. Some do.

> *"This [obesity] is an epidemic in the US the likes of which we have not had before in chronic disease" (Dietz 2001).*

You can probably see this happening. If you look at old high school yearbooks or class photos, for example, you can tell that, in the past, young people were hardly ever overweight. And your old yearbooks do not have to be all that old to show that the problem is accelerating. Why is this happening? You can see the causes all around you, as they affect your own life and as they affect the lives of your children.

As a parent, you'll find yourself blamed. You're the one who takes children to fast food restaurants, who lets the television do the babysitting, who won't cook a decent meal, who refuses to drive your children to a recreation center for an hour of active sports. Of course, you may or may not be guilty of the laziness that so many love to blame on you. Most parents actually do their best. And when they leave their children with caretakers, they make every effort to find professional workers who will do their best, too.

17

"Becoming obese is the normal response to the American environment"
(Hill 2000).

We want to make it clear that you probably don't need to worry about putting a baby or toddler on a diet as such. No child should be on a restricted-calorie diet, except in the most extreme and extraordinary cases. Baby fat is not really a risk.

A child who eats a basically good diet from the beginning and who has normal opportunities for play and exercise will probably grow up to be physically fit and at the right weight. A small child who seems too fat can usually grow into the excess weight by cutting out empty-calorie foods and playing vigorously.

The older the child the higher the risk of becoming overweight.

Of overweight children at ages four and five, only about 20 percent will grow up as overweight adults. But wait until the child is in junior high school, and the risk has risen to more than 75 percent.

"Our gene pool isn't changing. Rather, it's that our environment now supports fatness. Because our society encourages people to eat more and more and to exercise less and less, those people who are genetically predisposed to become fat will do so" (Wadden 1997).

Since fat is a risk as children grow up, what can you do to prevent problems now, before the trouble begins? Even if your baby appears fat, err on the side of good nutrition rather than fewer calories. A baby who is normally active and healthy should not cause concern, especially if you are breastfeeding. Cutting down on feedings of a small baby is no easy task, anyway, and it probably is not advisable.

In infancy there is a fine line between malnutrition and good nutrition. The underfed baby is at risk since the brain cells are still multiplying, and the covering (the myelin sheath) surrounding the nerve cells is being formed. You would not want to jeopardize your baby's health and intellectual development to promote thinness, when baby fat is only temporary, anyway. And fat cells do carry some value. They act as insulators, protecting the infant from temperature changes and helping in the regulation of body temperature. They are energy reserves that can be called on in times of illness and stress.

Infancy is a risky period to play around with diets. The growth of the complex nervous system is too important. Of course, stuffing a child with large amounts of food is not going to develop a super brain. And neither is it going to cause the baby to grow up any faster or better. No one wants to put development on the borderline because it's fashionable to be thin or because the neighbors brag about how advanced their babies are in size or development.

Keep a happy food atmosphere.

The one factor that will lead to obesity or its opposite, extreme problems with body image that can lead to anorexia and nervosa, is if food comes to dominate the life of a growing young person. A parent's concern can be part of the problem. Worry can create an atmosphere of anxiety and control. All too often, food becomes the issue in power struggles with toddlers—and then with older children and teenagers. One reason that human beings have survived and prospered as a species is that they tend to have extremely strong digestive systems.

If your baby's food is good from the beginning, you won't lose the battle with the forces of the outside world. You'll win, with your child growing up healthy, happy, and well nourished.

References

Dietz, William. Director of Nutrition at the Center for Disease Control. Quoted by Greg Critser. Let them eat fat: the heavy truths about american obesity. *Harper's* March 2000.

Hill, James O. University of Colorado. Quoted by Greg Critser, Let them eat fat: the heavy truths about american obesity. *Harper's* March 2000.

Wadden, Thomas, PhD. University of Pennsylvania School of Medicine. Quoted in Joseph C. Piscatella, *Fat-Proof Your Child.* New York, New York: Workman, 1997.

Part Two

Choices, Decisions & Strategies

Chapter Five
Choose the Best Milk for Your Baby

When you breastfeed your baby, you do what is right for your baby. You do what's right for yourself. And you do what's right for the environment. You may even influence others, so more babies will benefit. When you nurse your baby, you take the kind and wise action of providing your baby with the best nature has to offer. Unfortunately, you may sometimes find that you do so in a hostile atmosphere.

In the last few years, women have been discriminated against and harassed for breastfeeding. In one or two odd cases, a woman has had her baby taken away from her and put into foster care because she breastfed longer than society thought was acceptable. A few women have been asked to leave public establishments as if breastfeeding constituted some sort of indecent exposure. In a society where breasts (and women themselves) can be viewed as totally sexual objects, then a nursing mother can appear to be breaking the laws against indecent behavior.

Of course, you can imagine that government agencies and medical authorities support breastfeeding, at least on paper. But did you realize that among the supporters of nursing mothers is none other than *Playboy* magazine? A possibly deranged or at least eccentric reader wrote in that his wife was insisting on nursing their newborn baby, even though he viewed her breasts as belonging to him. Her breasts were his sexual fantasy, not intended for practical use. In their startlingly feminist reply, the editors of the magazine clearly viewed him as getting his priorities all wrong.

Government agencies do pay lip service to breastfeeding initiatives. Yet more money is all too often spent on infant formula than promotion of breastfeeding. The United States government, for example, provides free formula to many babies born into low-income families and spends millions of dollars a year to do so.

The rise of the formula industry.

The formula industry is a hugely profitable enterprise. Over the last decade, formula sales have tripled. The formula manufacturers take in as much as $22 million in revenues every day. That's every day. Their marketing experts say they're only just beginning, too. They're not even close to reaching market saturation.

These are major manufacturers, with the usual modern pattern of giant corporations owned by even more giant corporations. Currently, Enfamil dominates baby formula sales. That company is Mead Johnson, owned by the even larger Bristol-Myers Squibb Company. The major competition is Ross Laboratories, a division of Abbott Laboratories, and manufacturing Similac and the soymilk formula, Isomil. A contender is Wyeth, under the ownership of American Home Products. An outside observer can be forgiven for getting the idea that these corporate entities spend more energy buying and selling one another than they do in improving their products. And they spend more time on marketing and advertising than on actual improvements.

The companies' attempts at research tend to focus on comparing different sorts of formula, presumably with the purpose of showing the superiority of their own products over the competition. In their publicity and advertising, they do acknowledge the superiority of human milk. That's a given.

The move to marketing formula as if it were soap.

The Infant Feeding Action Committee, INFACT Canada, accuses these companies of marketing what they term "artificial baby milks," as if they were detergents. (INFACT Canada is the North American representative of IBFAN, the International Baby Food Action Network. Look for the INFACT website at www.infactcanada.ca). How could such a marketing push come to seem acceptable on something as important as feeding babies? Strangely enough, this opportunity for profit began as almost an accident.

Back in the early part of the twentieth century, there were humanitarian efforts to help out mothers and babies who were in trouble. Social service agencies established milk banks, where the lucky mothers with plentiful milk supplies could give their milk to help out the less fortunate. But the organized milk banks were not sanitary enough, and the supply was uncertain. There were real problems then, as there have been real problems throughout human history, for sick babies, small orphans, and malnourished mothers. Then, as now, many babies could not thrive on milk from cows or goats.

Then, during World War II, many women were working in the factories and military service, so that the demand surged for artificial feeding. The burgeoning dairy industry seized upon a profit opportunity. Milk and milk products had been developing into an actual industry, more and more removed from local farms. Milk could be transported farther, stored longer, and sold at a higher profit than ever before. Milk was becoming a substance to be processed, packaged, and marketed.

The rise and fall and rise of breastfeeding.

The mothers of America presented good targets. Bottle-feeding seemed scientific and modern. By the 1950s, only about a quarter of all mothers were still breast-feeding when they left the hospital. The percentage rose in the 1960s and 1970s, with the rise of national advocacy groups such as La Leche League International. Young mothers had come to view breastfeeding as an interesting, almost counter-cultural move. But the number of nursing mothers dropped again in the 1980s and 1990s, as exhausted women entered a predominantly hostile and unbending work-force. Americans are used to technology, and they do tend to turn for help to the technology of bottles and formula.

In 1999, just over 67 percent of all new mothers in the USA started out breast-feeding their newborn babies. Six months later, more than 30 percent were still breastfeeding. By one year, the percentage of babies still receiving human milk is higher than in any recent year, about 17 percent (Ross Products/Abbott Laboratories survey 1999).

Who is breastfeeding?

The statistical profile of the nursing mother shows her as past her teen years—in her 20s and 30s—with more than one child. She often has a college education. She has a middle-class income. No government program supports her directly or helps her baby. The American nursing mother lives in the Western states, where, historically, breastfeeding is favored. She is most likely to receive strong support from family, friends, and medical advisors.

Although more new mothers are currently breastfeeding, and the statistics are encouraging, the fact remains that babies born to financially well-off families are also the most likely to receive the additional advantages of mother's milk. (Consider, also, that breastfeeding saves about $1,800 over a baby's first year. That's not even counting that bottle-fed babies are statistically more prone to illness in the first year than breastfed babies, and their parents may run up more medical bills.)

One way of looking at these statistics is that those who are bottle-feeding are those who can least afford it. They're young, inexperienced, possibly low-income and not well educated. They represent the most vulnerable people in our society. Often, they suffer from low self-esteem. Although these women want the best for their babies, they find it difficult to analyze the options and to make a strong, sometimes counter-cultural decision. Often, their own mothers and other women they know are used to bottles. The older generation does not know how to help and support a nursing mother in the younger generation. Despite a few strong local initiatives, those women who need the most help and support for their babies are apparently—for the most part—getting the least.

The statistical fact is that, when other things have gone wrong for a baby, breastfeeding is sometimes a matter of life and death. If all mothers—especially the most needy—could breastfeed for just two or three months, the infant mortal-ity rate in the United States would decline by just under five percent (Baumslag and Michaels 1995). You can see that's not a huge percentage. At first glance, it's not an impressive statistic. But it is real human lives.

Putting on the golden handcuffs.

Most hospitals do not support breastfeeding as well as they could. Most hospitals in North America accept donations of thousands of dollars of free formula from the major formula manufacturers. One nurse at the Boston Medical Center in Boston, Massachusetts, calls this money the "golden handcuffs." The hospitals get their formula for free, and the companies also provide a free formula packet for each new mother and baby—plus they throw in all the advertising hospitals are willing to display, even to the Enfamil or Similac logo on the pink or blue souvenir name cards on the babies' bassinets.

For the record, the formula companies say they are not doing this to discourage breastfeeding. They say they are only trying to influence the mother's choice of brand. They term their in-hospital advertising as "promotional" (certainly) and "educational" (hardly).

Throwing off the golden handcuffs.

Now a few medical centers are aggressively improving their breastfeeding programs. They buy their own formula and other supplies, instead of depending on the freebies. They put up posters encouraging breastfeeding instead of the advertisements. They counsel mothers with good advice. And they allow the new babies to room near their mothers, where the nursing couple can learn together what is best for the new life.

Is your hospital baby-friendly?

The United Nations and the World Health Organization confer the name "Baby Friendly" on hospitals that meet their standards for helping mothers to breastfeed their babies. As of the year 2000, there were 14,800 Baby Friendly hospitals in the world. Only 27 of them were in the United States.

Formula as third-world killer.

If the United States and Canada have had difficulty maintaining breastfeeding rates, Third World countries have been in even worse trouble. Formula companies promote their product, with an initial free supply, to mothers who don't live in an environment in which bottle-feeding is safe. The marketing push for formula is, all too often, targeting those who are already living in poverty. The expense of formula could seriously deprive the rest of the family. Most pathetically, older children sometimes steal formula out of their own hunger. Or families have had to stretch out their supply of formula by diluting it excessively. Even then, many families have no clean water to mix into formula. The instructions are often in English or French only, so that the parents cannot read the instructions. In the past, salespeople even entered the hospital, and visited mothers in their homes, sometimes dressed as if they were medical authorities.

By 1981, the situation in the Third World had become so desperate that the World Health Assembly adopted the International Code of Marketing of Breast Milk Substitutes. That code helped in some countries, although there have been continuous violations. (To read more about the politics of breastfeeding and formula sales, see *Milk, Money, and Madness: The Culture and Politics of Breastfeeding* (Baumslag and Michels 1995).

Mother's milk as a form of wealth.

Breastfeeding is an important natural resource everywhere, among rich or poor. In a wealthy country, the mother who bottle-feeds is wasting resources. She is spending extra money, using up extra milk, extra hot water, and, often, disposable bottles. She is throwing away her own good milk. But the waste is not ordinarily a matter of life and death. In some parts of the world, however, mother's milk has actually been counted as a form of national wealth. Where food is scarce, the human mother is an important source of nourishment. It's a natural resource.

Authorities who recommend breastfeeding for the first one or two years of a baby's life:

- The World Health Organization
- UNICEF
- The American Academy of Pediatrics
- The Canadian Paediatric Society
- The Paediatric Society in New Zealand
- The National Breastfeeding Committee in Germany
- La Leche League International
- The Quran (Koran)
- The Bible

The grand inconsistency of human milk.

Mass-produced formula is consistent and uniform in its ingredients. That's only right for a commercial product. Human milk, on the other hand, changes as the baby changes. In a way, breastfeeding is a continuation of pregnancy. A mother's body provides for the varying needs of the fetus as it develops, and lactation serves the same purpose. It's different milk for a baby who is one hour old than for a child who is one year old, old enough to eat other foods and to lose some of the early dependence on mother's milk.

Science has to have its limits when it comes to duplicating all that. We can't grow a baby in a decanter (not just yet anyway), and we can't formulate perfect human milk.

Benefits of the first milk.

New milk for a newborn baby is called colostrum. For most animals, colostrum is a life-or-death matter. Human beings can survive without it, but it has immense benefits.

In the first days after birth, colostrum helps to clean out the immature digestive system. It provides extra immunities against disease.

After the first few days, the colostrum gradually gives way to the mother's milk that is meant to nourish the baby through the first months of growth.

Human milk looks thinner than formula or cow's milk. It's almost translucent and has a bluish tone. It does not look as rich and creamy as formula or cow's milk. It doesn't look like the white, thick milk we're accustomed to seeing. So some people get the impression that formula is providing something extra. But this is an illusion. That thin, bluish milk is really contributing much more (and in some good ways, less) than formula and cow's milk could provide.

Both colostrum and mature human milk contain antibodies that protect infants from intestinal disease and diarrhea at a time when they are most vulnerable. The breastfed baby runs less risk of intestinal infection during the first year. There's less risk of diaper rash because the stool is acidic, and the acid discourages the growth of bacteria that cause rashes. Cow's milk, on which most formula is based, produces a neutral to alkaline stool in which these bacteria multiply.

> *"Many medical professionals admit that they withhold breastfeeding information from mothers so the women won't feel guilty if they choose not to do it (women are seen as needing protection from knowing the possible consequences of making a poor choice)"* (Baumslag and Michels 1995).

Splendid advantages for breastfed babies.

- During the nursing period, breastfed babies have fewer illnesses than do bottle-fed babies. Human milk stimulates the immune system. They tend to suffer fewer staph infections. They are less liable to catch common influenza, ear infections, colds, and other respiratory infections. If they do come down with an illness, it may be less severe than it might have been.

- Statistically, bottle-fed babies suffer eczema or allergy-associated skin irritation seven times as often as breastfed babies.

- An important benefit of human milk is this lower incident of allergies. Babies are never allergic to human milk, but they frequently develop allergies to cow's milk.

- Breastfed babies tend to be normal weight. Or if they do get fat, they usually stabilize their weight without difficulty by the time they are

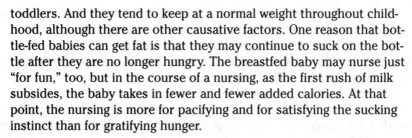

toddlers. And they tend to keep at a normal weight throughout child-hood, although there are other causative factors. One reason that bot-tle-fed babies can get fat is that they may continue to suck on the bot-tle after they are no longer hungry. The breastfed baby may nurse just "for fun," too, but in the course of a nursing, as the first rush of milk subsides, the baby takes in fewer and fewer added calories. At that point, the nursing is more for pacifying and for satisfying the sucking instinct than for gratifying hunger.

- One recent study indicates that breastfed babies are more likely to have the right blood pressure when they are adults, even if they were breastfed for only a short period.

- Dental studies show that babies fed at the breast develop fewer prob-lems with their future teeth than do bottle-fed babies. Breastfeeding is work for the baby, and the natural sucking develops the baby's mouth, jaw, and gums in the right way. The work helps prevent maloc-clusion in the baby's orthodontic future.

- A breastfed baby may grow to be more accepting of a wide range of new foods. There is no way to research this scientifically, but the the-ory is that you may well avoid the transition stage when toddlers often become picky and cranky about food and sometimes insist on an extremely restricted diet. The idea is that breastfed babies are exposed to many smells and flavors from the mother's diet. They're subtly transmitted through human milk.

- Some authorities have even advanced the theory that breastfed babies have better visual function and learn better. Good visual and cognitive development may be associated with fatty acids available only in human milk.

- Breastfeeding is a first social experience. It builds and strengthens the bond between mother and child, the first love between one human being and another.

Of course, it is difficult to isolate breastfeeding as a single, simple cause in the intellectual, social, and physical development of babies. It is one factor in the many complexities of child development.

Why isn't unmodified cow's milk—or often, milk-based for-mula—good for a human baby?

Right after birth, a calf can stagger to its feet and find its milk. In a few months, it has all the education it needs to be bovine or bullish, as the case may be. Big Mama Cow is giving her baby protein enough—more than three times the protein of human milk—so that, in two years, the calf will be all grown up.

Human milk, in contrast, contains nearly twice the carbohydrates of cow's milk. After all, it's for a baby who does not need to be running around the meadow two weeks after birth. Instead, the human baby needs to complete a complicated nervous system and, with luck, a powerful brain. The carbohydrate and fat content of human milk allow that sort of slow, complex growth.

Human milk and cow's milk have about the same fat content, 3.5 percent to 3.8 percent. The fat in human milk is more digestible and is more readily absorbed by human babies, however, and contains the right balance of fatty acids for completing the central nervous system.

Obviously, human beings are tough animals. They've taken over the world. One physical reason is that their digestive systems can tolerate abuse. Even the immature digestive system of an infant can usually put up with cow's milk, at least at some point. But an infant's digestive and metabolic systems must work hard to cope with the excessive protein of cow's milk. The excess protein puts stress on the baby's kidneys. The curd form is larger and harder in cow's milk and therefore less digestible. And whole cow's milk protein can cause slight bleeding in the intestines which can lead to a form of anemia.

If you have a family history of diabetes, your baby is at risk for diabetes later in life and should not be given cow's milk proteins in the first year or more.

In commercial formula, cow's milk is modified to resemble human milk, and it's safer than plain cow's milk. The protein in formula is changed so that it will form a softer curd in baby's stomach and will digest more easily.

Carbohydrates are increased to proportions similar to those in mother's milk, and the formula is fortified with vitamins and minerals, usually including iron. The result is that the bottle-fed baby may well be getting much more iron than the breastfed baby. But the iron in human milk is in a much more physically usable form, suitable to the infant digestive system.

Plain cow's milk contains about four times the natural salt of human milk, so formula manufacturers must reduce the salt as well.

In addition, the amino acid "building blocks" of the cow's milk protein are a different type and are in different proportions. (The amino acid in cow's milk is mostly casein; in human milk, it is mostly lactalbumin.) Essentially, nature intends the amino acids in cow's milk to spur the growth of muscle and fat tissue. The amino acids in human milk spur the growth of the brain.

The formula companies are still tinkering with the amino acid problem and occasionally add or modify one of the fatty acids in cow's milk, in an attempt to make it more like human milk. Since the amino acids are so basically important, that's a critical sort of tinkering. Giving your baby human milk means not having to worry about whether the formula companies ever get the amounts and types just right.

Less critically, cow's milk or cow's milk formula forms an odorous stool. To be blunt, breastfed babies smell better than bottle-fed babies.

It is not that the formula producers have failed to create satisfactory substitutes for human milk. They have identified most of the critical components of human milk, and they do a good job of modifying cow's milk insofar as it can be modified. But they have other motives, besides the health of infants. Presumably,

ey want the best modifications, but they also want the least expensive. They
eed to make a profit as well as to feed babies.

And after all, they can't create human milk out of cow's milk any more than
ey could make a living tree out of scrap lumber.

The benefits of breastfeeding to mothers:

- Stimulation of contractions of the uterus that help stop bleeding and
  return the uterus to pre-pregnancy shape.

- Less risk of urinary tract infections in the weeks following childbirth.

- Easier loss of weight gained during pregnancy, as producing milk for
  the baby can require 500 to 800 extra calories per day.

- A delay in the return of her menstrual periods for six months or
  longer after the baby's birth, with very little chance of becoming pregnant during that time.

- Hormonal enhancement to feelings of bonding with the baby.

- Less risk of breast or ovarian cancer, even years later.

- Time to relax and to enjoy a naturally pleasurable experience.

- A feeling of confidence in her abilities and adequacy as a mother.

- Savings of her time, effort, and money.

reparing for breastfeeding during pregnancy.

he best time to prepare for breastfeeding is during pregnancy. Here's how to pre-
:nt a few problems or at least reduce their severity:

- Don't use soap on your nipples during pregnancy or after the baby is
  born. Warm water is adequate for cleaning.

- Occasionally, nipples may be flat or they may be inverted so that they
  turn inward when you try to pull them out. When a nursing baby pulls
  on them, they can become sore. You may be able to troubleshoot this
  problem during pregnancy by wearing hollow plastic breast shields
  designed to create a light, almost unnoticeable suction that, before
  the baby is born, pulls the nipples out little by little.

- A support bra or nursing bra may add to your comfort in the last
  months of pregnancy.

reastfeeding the newborn baby.

- When the baby is born, nurse as early and as often as you can. Many
  mothers nurse the baby right after delivery, ideally in the first hour.
  Nursing reassures the baby about this new world.

- Don't worry if a newborn baby doesn't nurse right away. A newborn baby may be too exhausted or too sleepy or, once in a while, too agitated to nurse. The natural instincts will come along in time.

- Find a comfortable place to nurse, with pillows and armrests at the right angles. You don't want to add muscle fatigue to the other discomforts of giving birth.

- Have a nursing expert show you the right position for your baby to nurse.

- Fold handkerchiefs or use nursing pads inside your bra to guard against milk leakage during the first few days. Soon you will have the right amount of milk for your baby and leakage will not be a round-the-clock problem. But especially with a first baby, nature is sometimes overenthusiastic. Just don't use anything plastic.

- Don't believe the every-four-hours convention of baby feeding. Successful breastfeeding depends upon frequency and length of nursing. As babies nurse, they are establishing and guaranteeing their milk supply. They are bringing in milk. You may get the impression in the first few weeks that your baby intends to bring in enough milk for triplets. The baby is just intending to be a survivor.

- Nurse on one side for as long as baby is actively sucking and swallowing and then switch to the other side. Reverse the order the next time.

- Stick with it. In the first days after birth, a new mother's breasts sometimes swell with milk and the other fluids involved in getting the milk started. The breasts can be large and hard at first, and if the nipples are flat, it's like asking the baby to nurse a basketball. It's frustrating, to say the least. However, engorgement or sore nipples improve within days, sometimes even more quickly. And after a few days, the letdown reflex operates only when you need it. Before long, your baby will be sleeping for tolerably long periods of time.

- If you run into difficulties, ask for help. Check the Resources section for ways to get in touch with La Leche League International.

Breastfeeding during the first few months.

- Don't use formula supplements. Breastfeeding is like few other enterprises in the world: You get out of it exactly what you put into it. Babies produce milk in proportion to need, and they bring it in by the length of time and the energy they spend nursing. If you use a formula supplement, it will cut down on the baby's nursing time and keep your milk supply from building up. In the first weeks, you should expect eight to twelve feedings every 24 hours.

- The best way to build up the milk supply is by repeated nursing.
- Insofar as possible, avoid medication that is not essential. That includes over-the-counter painkillers and mega-vitamins. If you must take prescription medicine, consult your doctor about the effects on your baby, and get in touch with La Leche League International for additional information.
- Nurse on both breasts with each feeding in the early weeks. The composition of the milk changes as nursing goes on, with the thinner milk first, followed by creamier milk with higher fat content later in the feeding. An experienced mother can almost feel the change in the milk. The baby slows feeding and gradually loses interest. But if put to the other breast, the baby often begins nursing again with more enthusiasm.

How to tell if your baby is getting enough milk.

- You can hear sounds of swallowing.
- After the first few days of life, your baby is eager to nurse every two to three hours. Your baby is nursing at least ten to twenty minutes per breast.
- After the first few days of life, your baby is producing five or six wet diapers a day.
- The urine has no significant color or odor.
- After the first few days of life, your baby is producing two to five bowel movements a day. After the first six weeks or so, your baby's bowel movements may become less frequent.
- After the first few days, your baby is gaining weight and size.
- After the first week or so, your baby's skin is not extraordinarily dry.
- The skin springs back immediately after a gentle pinch.

Breastfeeding while away from your baby.

- Get all the help and support you can, both logistically and emotionally. Human milk is the perfect nourishment for babies, and you don't want to give that up as soon as you encounter a problem.
- If you must be away from your baby for several hours a day, you can still provide the benefits of mother's milk. One way is to use a pump or express milk by hand every few hours, and store it in sterilized bottles for a caretaker to give the baby. Then you can nurse the baby yourself when you are together, perhaps planning extra time for that purpose. Expressing milk helps keep up your milk supply around the clock. You may need some practice at first, but a routine can be workable.

- The frequency with which you need to express milk depends on the age of the baby and other factors, such as cooperation from your employer. But many working mothers are able to express milk three times at work, during a morning break, at noon, and then during an afternoon break. As the baby grows older, a mother can plan to express milk less frequently.

- A hospital-style electric pump may be appropriate for the mother who needs to create milk artificially over a long period of time, as when a baby is ill or premature and unable to suckle normally. A hospital or medical rental agency can rent one to you, and medical insurance may cover the cost.

- A larger pump often has the advantage of a natural automatic suck-release cycle. Small electric pumps provide continuous action. A double pump also has the advantage of saving time and stimulating the breasts more effectively. A mother can finish pumping in ten to fifteen minutes.

- Store mother's milk in sterilized bottles, made of heavy plastic or glass. Or you can buy special milk bags for the purpose. Do not use the sort of disposable bottle liners that are intended to hold formula.

- Mother's milk can be stored in the refrigerator at 32 to 39 degrees Fahrenheit (24 to 32 degrees Celsius) for up to eight days. Or freeze the milk in the freezer compartment of a home refrigerator for two weeks or so or in a separate freezer for up to 12 months.

- If you are away at your job all day, consider having the baby brought to you. A few socially responsible companies arrange for child care on the premises, so that you can visit your child several times a day. This is a time for creative thinking about a routine that allows you both the benefits of breastfeeding to you and your baby—and also gives you a reasonable chance to earn a living.

For more about the art and science of breastfeeding, consult La Leche League International at www.lalecheleague.org or their classic THE WOMANLY ART OF BREASTFEEDING.

Breastfeeding as the baby grows older.

- As your child is able to eat a variety of foods, continue to breastfeed first. For the first year of life, there is no food superior to human milk. So give your priority to the best nourishment.

- Breastfeeding a toddler is considered normal in many societies. It continues the emotional and physical advantages to both you and your child. More women breastfeed for a longer time—two years or more—than you might think. They just may not be talking about it outside of support groups such as La Leche League International.

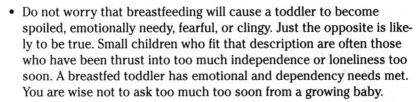

- Do not worry that breastfeeding will cause a toddler to become spoiled, emotionally needy, fearful, or clingy. Just the opposite is likely to be true. Small children who fit that description are often those who have been thrust into too much independence or loneliness too soon. A breastfed toddler has emotional and dependency needs met. You are wise not to ask too much too soon from a growing baby.

- Ideally, a baby should be the one to initiate weaning. The growing toddler gradually forgets about nursing, without a feeling of loss or distress. A toddler gets too busy to lie around drinking milk. Any weaning that must be done before the child reaches that stage of natural readiness ought to be done slowly, gradually, and with love.

- Reduce nursing gradually for your own comfort as well as the baby's. An abrupt weaning can be painful to the mother. If the mother is ill, it might be better for her to find a way to keep on nursing than to combine her illness with the additional stress of an abrupt weaning.

Giving bottles, if necessary.

If your child care provider needs to give mother's milk in a bottle, here are some rules to make it as safe as possible.

- When you feed the baby, make sure the milk comes from the nipple drop by drop so the baby will not get it too fast. A small baby can choke easily.

- Do not let the baby lie flat while bottle-feeding. None of us could drink well from that position.

- Plan to take at least twenty minutes to give a bottle. It is important to satisfy a baby's sucking instincts with a long, slow, emotionally satisfying feeding, just as a nursing mother does.

- Hold the baby on alternate sides for each feeding, just as you would if you were nursing. You will be helping the baby's eyes to coordinate, among other benefits.

- Never prop a bottle. Propping is not safe, since you might not be right there if the baby choked or otherwise ran into trouble. If a baby takes a going-to-sleep bottle in bed, the milk may ferment in the baby's mouth all night long. Bottles of milk, formula, or juice given at night in this way are a major cause of tooth decay in small children. All-night sucking on an artificial nipple is also not conducive to correct development of the mouth and teeth.

How to warm the milk.

- Always warm human milk to body temperature. Don't fail to test some drops on your wrist before you offer it to the baby.
- Do not use a microwave oven to heat the milk.
- Do not bring human milk to a boil.
- The best way to thaw frozen milk or to heat refrigerated milk is to hold the container under warm, running water. You may also heat a pan of water on the stove and immerse the container of milk in the heated water.

Decide on iron or vitamin supplements for your baby.

Supplements are a decision you must make with your medical advisor. Your baby is unique, so you may not wish to make the same decisions you hear others make. Here are some factors to consider:

About iron supplements

Too much iron for too young a baby can cause constipation. It can also interfere with some of the protective aspects of human milk.

A healthy, full-term baby is born with enough iron to last about the first six months of life, or until the baby doubles birth weight. Mother's milk has low levels of iron, but the iron is more available and usable for the infant body than is the iron from formula or food supplements. So, ordinarily, you will not need to consider iron supplements for the first six months or so of your baby's life.

Most authorities, including the American Academy of Pediatrics, recommend supplementary iron by the time a baby is about six months of age, often in combination with vitamin C. Since most six-month-old babies are ready for food other than mother's milk, iron can often be in the form of iron-fortified cereal, fruits, vegetables, and meats.

About vitamin supplements

Remember that if a nursing mother is taking vitamin supplements, her baby is receiving them though her milk. Human milk is the perfect nourishment for a human baby, and very few babies under that age of six months need supplements of any sort.

Authorities have been concerned recently about a because they are seeing rickets and other problems caused by a deficiency of vitamin D. This problem is particularly serious among babies who are sun-deprived because they live in an extreme northern climate, have dark skin, are dressed in layers of clothing that prevent sunshine from getting through, or stay indoors to avoid extremely hot temperatures. Just a few minutes a day exposing a baby's cheeks to the sun can solve the problem.

When the baby is old enough, a fortified cereal and fortified milk will also help to provide enough vitamin D (and other vitamins). The emphasis on using sunscreen to protect baby from harmful effects of sunlight may also be contributing to this problem by interfering with the baby's absorption of vitamin D.

The time will come for milk in a cup.

Many advisers are telling parents to wait on cow's milk of any sort until the baby is one year old. The risk of infant milk allergy is high, perhaps as high as seventy percent, for babies under one year old. Almost all children outgrow milk allergy by the time they are two or three years old. Milk allergy in preschool children is only about five percent.

If you do decide to begin giving your baby the same milk as the rest of the family, watch out for symptoms of allergy in the form of repeated respiratory illness: wheezing, runny nose, earaches. Also, look out for any red, rough facial rash. Early milk allergy can set a child up for a future milk allergy.

Here are some ways to problem-shoot any possible milk allergy:

- Begin yogurt and cottage cheese first. These foods are usually safe when your baby is about nine months old.

- Begin milk just a bit at a time, just a few sips a day. Do not give milk as the primary drink.

Yet children tend to like the taste and texture of milk better than other foods and drinks. They're used to milk, and they usually take to the family milk readily.

The ideal way to begin milk is in a beginner's trainer "sippy" cup. The baby who is old enough to drink milk with the rest of the family ought to be old enough to sit up and hold the cup with both hands. Pour in just a small amount of milk at first, especially since you may be wiping up a spill any time.

Begin with whole milk. Low-fat milk (2 percent fat) is generally all right when your baby is between 18 and 24 months old, especially if that's what the rest of the family drinks.

Mother's milk is the baby's survival emotionally as well as physically.

Nursing a baby is a privilege. A nursing mother is the loved one that the baby first connects with and is reliant on for nourishment and survival. She is the means by which her baby survives. From her, the baby learns to react to people and to socialize with a father, siblings, grandparents, aunts and uncles, caretakers—and a friendly passerby or two.

As months go on, the baby reaches out to give those loved parents and caregivers some food. Your baby hands you a soggy cookie, or attempts to put the spoon into your mouth.

Then the parents can know they've won. It's an infant thank-you. It's the first reciprocal gesture. It's the rest of the life ceremony that you begin with the first nursing.

Your child has come around to knowing who you are and why you're there.

References

Baumslag, Naomi and Dia L. Michels. *Milk, Money, and Madness: The Culture and Politics of Breastfeeding.* Westport, Connecticut: Bergin and Garvey, 1995.

La Leche League International THE WOMANLY ART OF BREASTFEEDING Schaumburg, Illinois: LLLI, 1997. www.lalecheleague.org

Chapter Six
Choose the Best Water and Juice

Your baby is mostly water. In fact, more than 70 percent of a baby's body is water. Adults are less watery, with bodies of just over 50 percent water.) Water flows through the body in various forms. It delivers nutrients and carries away waste. It cools and heats the body. It keeps skin supple, lubricates joints, keeps eyes functioning, and makes muscles work smoothly. Even a brain is mostly water. So, of course, your child needs plenty of water to grow and thrive. In an age of heavily sweetened, high-calorie beverages, you will be doing your children a great service if you encourage them to enjoy drinking water from an early age.

During the first six months of life, a healthy breastfed baby requires no extra water. A good time to start regular drinks of water for a baby is at the same time you start solids. Food goes down better for anyone with a few sips of water. At that time, you can begin water in a trainer "sippy" cup, rather than a bottle.

Here are some ways to make sure the water is pure enough for a baby (or anyone else, for that matter):

- Consider a filter. You can buy a convenient type with a pitcher attached. Just put tap water through the filter and refrigerate. Other types attach to a faucet.

- Consider a whole-house-activated carbon filter, especially if you have reason to be concerned about bacteria or chemicals in well water or the public water supply.

- Find out about how hard or soft your well or public water is. Hard water is "hard" because of the high level of minerals, including calcium and magnesium. Soft water, with its lower level of minerals, has a higher concentration of sodium. If you are able to make a choice, hard water is better for drinking because of the lower salt content.

- If you buy bottled water, remember that it is not necessarily a guarantee of purity. Look for water bottled from a natural spring and without added flavoring.

Older children may enjoy drinking water with ice, with a splash of lemon or lime as flavoring, or some seltzer. That's certainly preferable to the soft drinks that children and teenagers drink so much.

By the time a baby is about seven months old, you ought to be able to begin juices, as well as water, in a cup. Begin with a mild unsweetened fruit juice: apple, apricot, white grape, or pear. You probably should not try orange juice, grapefruit, and other citrus juices until the baby is over one year old. Citrus is a common allergen and the acidity of citrus juices could present an additional problem. Wait for a year before you give tomato juice, too, since tomatoes are also a common allergen.

Dilute the juice. For a beginner, dilute one fluid ounce (2 tablespoons or 30 milliliters) juice with three ounces (1/3 cup or 90 milliliters) water. After you are sure your baby is tolerating juice, you can dilute it less, half juice and half water. You may wish to continue to dilute juice with water. Many adults prefer to dilute some types of juice. Dilution reduces the sugar, and adults often like a lighter, less sugary taste.

Fresh, home-created juice is best. When you squeeze or process fruits or vegetables in a juicer, be sure to wash them first to remove any contaminants. Then pour the juice through a strainer to remove any remaining seeds or shreds. You can pasteurize fresh juice by boiling for about three minutes in order to kill bacteria.

When you buy juice, look for pure 100 percent juice with no added sugar. Buy pasteurized juices. Do not allow a small child to have cola or other soft drinks. You and the rest of the family may have to give up having sweet, carbonated drinks available at home, and you may have to give up drinking them in front of children. That may be a sacrifice that's ultimately good for you and keeps your child from using you as a negative role model.

Refrigerate all juices. Once a container is open, plan to use it or discard it within a few days.

Babies and toddlers tend to have a strong liking for juice. They naturally like sweet foods and drinks. (Studies have shown that even before birth, a baby reacts positively to a sweet fluid and negatively to bitter or sour tastes. That instinctive reaction is probably an automatic response that avoids many poisons or contaminated foods.) Parents often like the convenience, and they may believe that juices are good and nutritious. Certainly, juice is part of good food for babies and toddlers. But you can overdo it, and many parents give children far too much juice, too often. Juice has its drawbacks:

- Juice can replace milk. Human milk, formula, and cow's milk are all far superior for children than juice.

- Juice in a bottle can become a habit. A toddler may want to carry a bottle of juice everywhere and sleep with a bottle of juice. That can cause cavities and poor dental development. In fact, all-night (and sometimes all-day) juice is the major cause of dental caries in small children. Ideally, you should introduce juice in a cup and never allow it in a bottle.

- Juice can replace fruits and vegetables. It is not a good substitute. Currently, average toddlers take in more than one-third of their combined consumption of fruits and vegetables just as juice.

- Juice contains sugar. Many commercial juices contain large amounts of refined sugar, and even pure juice contains natural sugars, mostly as fructose. No matter what form it takes, sugar still represents empty calories. Research has shown—not surprisingly—a direct correlation between the amount of juice a child drinks and the proportion of calories that the child receives from sugar.

- The intense sweet taste of juice can give a child the idea that all foods and drinks ought to be sweet and sugary and bland. So a child can be set up for a less-than-ideal diet in later years.

- Juice can cause diarrhea and other gastrointestinal problems.

- In some children, juice can be a factor in causing obesity. In a few susceptible children who drink juice almost to the exclusion of other nourishment, juice can be associated with a type of malnourishment, causing failure to thrive.

How much juice is too much?

- For ages six to twelve months, stay at four ounces (1/2 cup or 120 milliliters) per day.

- For toddlers and preschoolers, aim for six ounces (3/4 cup or 180 milliliters) per day.

- For school age children, do not exceed eight ounces (one cup or 240 milliliters) per day.

Chapter Seven
Begin the Best Foods at the Best Times

Do you have the fortitude to think about what your baby actually needs, rather than what the full force of the commercial world says? Do you have the courage to be different from that "ideal" parent featured in the baby food ads—and from the family and friends who may believe the commercial message is the right idea? Can you resist the brainwashing?

If so, then when you decide when and how to begin food for your baby, look at your own unique baby. Ignore the full-color magazine ads. Keep away from the fake, commercialized science. Don't pick up the free, full-color, attractive brochures, bought and paid for by commercial interests and, all too often, on display in respectable-sounding places such as a pediatrician's office.

Your baby is the true authority. Your baby can tell you just when supplemental food is a very good idea—and when the time has not yet come. Here are some signs that your baby is ready, physically and emotionally:

- Your baby is at least five to six months old.

- Your baby weighs at least fourteen pounds. Ideally, a baby who is ready for solids is at least double his birth weight.

- Your baby can sit up, with support. Your baby has control of his head and neck.

- Your baby has plenty of saliva to begin digestion of food.

- Your baby has the ability to transfer food from the front to the back of the mouth. Your baby's throat muscles have developed a stronger, more mature swallowing ability. Babies are born with a tongue-thrust reflex, so that their instinct is to push food outward and forward. That's survival instinct, so that the baby will not choke on food or other substances. This instinct disappears after about four months, when the baby has developed other options, such as chewing and swallowing.

43

- Your baby has a tooth or two. This should be at five to seven months old.

- Your baby is capable of refusing food. The ability of turning away and indicating a negative decision does not develop until the baby is about five months old.

- Your baby likes to imitate other people. Your baby is showing distinct interest in other people's food. Your baby reacts with interest to the sights, sounds, and odors of cooking.

- Your baby can reach and handle—and perhaps try to taste or eat—food, toys, and other objects.

- Your baby is not ill and has no rashes.

If you start solid foods too early, you may be taking risks:

- Your baby may gag on, choke on, or cough up solid food.

- You run the risk of decreasing your milk supply. Since human milk is perfect for human babies, then any other food is inferior. If you begin too early, you could be replacing superior nourishment with inferior nourishment. Even formula may be better than too-early solid foods.

- Your baby is not learning to eat only when hungry. A baby has control over how much human milk to take. Below a certain level of maturity, your baby does not have control over how much other food to take. A baby who must take in food and cannot indicate "no" in any way, is not learning to regulate intake of food. Perhaps as a result, early feeding has been associated with becoming overweight later on, even into adulthood.

- With too-early food, your baby runs an increased risk of allergic reactions. If you wait a while to serve the same food, your baby may never have an allergic reaction.

- With too-early food, your baby runs the risk of poor digestion and poor absorption of food. That's almost certain. At best, food given too early passes through his system undigested.

Warning: Early solids will NOT...

- Help your baby sleep through the night,

- Make your baby less fussy,

- Make your baby develop earlier or grow up faster,

- Provide superior nutrition.

How to begin feeding non-milk foods.

- Heat the food. Your baby is accustomed to body-temperature milk.

- Mix the food with water or with the milk that the baby already knows. At first, the food should be mostly water or milk. Stir to get rid of lumps.

- Do not use a bottle-type feeder. Your baby has important skills to learn, how to take in food, chew, and swallow.

- For first feedings, your baby should be sitting up in your lap or in a high chair.

- You may want to use your (clean) finger at first, instead of a spoon. That will feel less startlingly different to the baby. A first spoon should be small and rounded.

- Offer very little at first. This is just practice for a while.

- Offer a new food for breakfast or lunch. If your baby were to have an allergic reaction, you don't want it to happen in the middle of the night.

- Offer one food at a time. Start another new food only after four to seven days, when the baby has reacted well and has not developed any gastrointestinal distress, diarrhea, or rash.

- Keep mealtimes slow and cheerful.

- Encourage your baby to pick up the food or spoon. Around five months old, babies can hold objects or food only between fingers and the palm of the hand, without real use of thumbs. Later, around seven months old, the baby can begin using thumbs for picking up objects or food. By ten months or so, you'll see much more coordinated grasping and handling. So don't worry about messiness. Your baby needs to practice new skills.

- Allow for plenty of experimenting, drooling, dawdling, dripping, dropping, and playing.

- Be extremely careful to notice if your baby starts to choke or cough.

- Never leave a baby alone with food or drink and make sure your baby stays on your lap or in a baby chair. Toddlers like to run around with food or drink in hand but it's just not safe.

Decide on a schedule for new foods.

You don't need to worry too much about what foods you start on what schedule. In fact, you should stay flexible and watch how well your baby accepts new foods. A good schedule allows four to seven days between introductions of each new food. Some parents prefer to start with a bit of mashed banana. Some prefer warm cooked cereal. A few like to begin with mashed bits of sweet potato or avocado.

The process of starting new foods ought to take three to six months. It ought to be one at a time, slow and steady.

Equipment for making your own baby food

You really don't need any special cooking equipment. Many beginner foods can be cooked along with food for adults, but leaving out spices and other ingredients for which the baby is not ready. Many baby foods can be mashed with an implement as simple as a fork.

But if you want to consider some tools that may make baby food preparations more convenient or more fun, here are a few optional suggestions. All are good for preparing adult foods, too.

- A hand-cranked food mill
- A hand grinder
- A strainer
- Ice cube trays (for freezing purees in small serving-size cubes)
- A blender or food processor
- A meat thermometer
- A double boiler
- Plastic freezer bags or containers
- A slow cooker or soup pot
- A vegetable steamer

Chapter Eight
Grow Your Baby with Great Menus for Each Age

Good nourishment is a matter of balance. You balance each meal with foods that interact to fulfill a wide range of physical needs. The greater the variety of good foods, the more you can be assured of complete nourishment. As you begin non-milk foods for your growing baby, that's the goal. Keep in mind that until your baby is about a year old, your milk still provides the best source of nutrition and should continue as the baby's primary source of nourishment.

A sample starting schedule (beginning about the middle of the first year, when the baby is ready).

At first, you'll want to offer the breast before giving solids. Wait four to seven days between each step to make sure the baby is tolerating each new food. Once a new food is started, it should continue to be part of baby's menu on a regular basis.

Step One:

- Begin with a bit of banana for breakfast. Mash up a bit of ripe banana with a fork. Bananas are bland and smooth and they taste enough like milk that they won't surprise the baby too much. Bananas are good nutrition, with a supply of potassium, a very small amount of iron, and some vitamins A and C. Increase the amount of banana every day according to baby's appetite.

Step Two:

- After baby is accustomed to banana, you can add another new fruit or vegetable, such as mashed sweet potato, mashed avocado, cooked unsweetened applesauce, or pureed cooked carrots. Some babies who don't like banana can be given these foods first. Each new vegetable should be well cooked and soft. You may want to mash them with a fork or puree them in a blender, food processor, or food mill. Then as your baby develops eating skills, you can allow for more texture. Do not add salt, butter, or spices.

Step Three:

- Add a third new fruit or vegetable. You may want to offer baby some tastes of solids twice a day at this point but start new foods only at breakfast or lunch.

Step Four:

- One at a time, add other new fruits and vegetables.

- If your baby seems enthusiastic, expand to three meals a day—breakfast, lunch, and dinner.

Step Five:

- Add whole grain cereal. Cereal has long been the traditional first baby food for formula-fed infants. Cereal is a good addition if you are concerned about slow weight growth and want to add calories. Begin with rice or barley cereal since these grains are less liable to cause allergies than wheat. Use single whole grains only. Make your own. (See page 81.)

   If you use a commercial cereal, look for one specially formulated for babies. Look for whole grains, enriched, iron-fortified, and unsweetened. Mix with mashed banana, with water, or with the milk the baby already takes. Do not mix with whole cow's milk until baby is one year old. Do not give chunks of dry cereal to a baby under ten months old. Don't get your hopes up about cereal: It will not help your baby sleep through the night.

Step Six:

- Introduce a first meat, poultry, or legume. If you decide to introduce your baby to meat or poultry, make sure it is lean and very thoroughly cooked, without added salt. Do not use smoked meats. You may wish to puree the meat or poultry with added water or with a familiar fruit or vegetable. Good first offerings are chicken or lean beef. Or you may wish to try a few sips of simple, unsalted beef or chicken soup stock. If you prefer a vegetarian alternative, try tofu, peas, lentils, or kidney beans.

Step Seven:

- As your baby is developing new teeth and the ability to chew, you can start teething biscuits, breads, rice, and pasta.

- When your baby is able to eat each separate ingredient, you can offer complex foods such as baked goods, soups, stew, casseroles, and salads. The baby can start sharing family food, and you will no longer need to prepare special purees or different meals.

- Your baby may enjoy eating meals and snacks when other people are eating also.

Step Eight and onward:

- Along with other new foods, introduce fruit juice. Begin with apple, white grape, pear, or other non-citrus juice. Wait on orange juice until after your baby's first birthday.

- When baby is nine or ten months old you may want to introduce hard-cooked egg yolk. Eggs are one of the foods most liable to cause allergy, especially the egg white. So you may wish to delay whole eggs until after your baby's first birthday. Yet eggs are also a good source of nourishment and eventually you may want to give your baby eggs or egg yolk three times a week. If you decide on egg yolk, try a very small bit at a time.

- After one year, you can probably begin cow's milk, whole eggs, tomatoes, and other important foods. These foods are at high risk for allergic reactions, but they are basic foods that provide good nourishment, and they often become a child's favorites.

A Sample Menu after One Year

Breakfast
Fruit or juice
Egg, three times a week
Cereal or toast, whole grain, unsweetened
Mother's milk or other dairy choice

Lunch
Vegetable soup
Whole grain bread, spread with meat, cheese, or hummus
Fruit
Mother's milk or other dairy choice

Dinner
Serving of meat, poultry, fish, or legumes
Serving of rice, potatoes, pasta, or vegetables
Fresh vegetable or fruit salad
A fruit or milk-based dessert
Mother's milk or other dairy choice

Snacks
Raw vegetables and fruits
Whole-grain crackers and biscuits
Mother's milk or other dairy choice

Balanced meals for toddlers (and other people, too).

One way to look at menus for older babies and toddlers who are beginning to eat a variety of foods is to balance each meal:

- A main source of protein, such as meat, poultry, egg, or a non-meat combination of grains and vegetables
- A starch, such as potatoes, rice, or pasta
- One or two other sources of complex carbohydrates such as fruits and vegetables
- Milk, or other dairy product, for its protein, calcium, and good fats

To make sure you're getting it right, look at colors. The best foods are almost always a vibrant color. They're dark green (broccoli, spinach), red or dark red (tomatoes, kidney beans, strawberries), orange or dark yellow (sweet potato, carrot, apricot, oranges, peach), blue or purple (plums, grapes, cherries, blueberries). What the best foods are not is dull plain white, such as white flour or shortening. Bright artificial colors equal dull artificial flavors.

Labels everywhere announce "lower in fat." You may ask, "Lower than what?" But that question does not always have an answer. Another common trick is to lower the fat, but replace it with sugar. Look at almost any canned product, such as soup, that claims to sell you vegetables. It's also selling you salt, sugar, and chemical additives.

The best protein foods.

Protein is the basic nourishment. Take away the substantial water of which each of us is made, and the rest is almost all protein. Our organs, muscles, bones, blood, skin, just about everything is protein. Our enzymes, hormones, and other chemicals are all built of protein. As everything in our bodies is constantly being used up or worn away, it is also constantly being repaired and replaced. Children need protein to build and grow. So a growing child needs a greater proportion of protein in food than adults do.

Protein is made up of complex combinations of amino acids. The body is capable of generating many of the amino acids it needs. Other amino acids cannot be made in our bodies and must come from amino acids in food. All animal-based foods, including milk, eggs, and meat contain complete proteins. They contain all of the amino acids a person needs from food. Plant-based foods also provide protein, but it is generally incomplete, without all the amino acids a person needs through food. Vegetarians combine various plant-based foods to create complete protein needs. So a good combination of vegetables and grains provide all the amino acids a person needs.

The best sources of protein:

- Lean beef
- Fish
- Dairy products
- Tofu and other soy products

- Legumes, such as beans and lentils
- Eggs
- Nuts

The best complex carbohydrate foods.

Carbohydrates are the principal source of fuel for the body. Most carbohydrate foods convert into glucose and circulate through the blood to all the cells in the body, providing energy. When a body's glucose level is not right, the body is in trouble.

Although most parts of the body can metabolize proteins and fats, carbohydrates are the first to supply energy. All too many of us get most of our carbohydrates from refined sugar. That's a simple carbohydrate that provides nothing more than the calories to supply energy. Sugar is so simple that it passes into the bloodstream very readily and can create problems with the glucose level. On the other hand, complex carbohydrates such as those in vegetables and fruits provide actual nourishment as well as energy, including fiber, a small amount of protein, vitamins, and minerals. The body assimilates the complex carbohydrates slowly and gradually—and with less negative consequence.

We're complex creatures and we need complex foods, such as these best complex carbohydrates:

- Beans, chickpeas, lentils, peas
- Oatmeal
- Tofu, soy flour, and other soy products
- Sweet potatoes
- Whole-grain cereals, pastas, and flours
- Brown rice
- Other vegetables and fruits

Sweet ways to avoid sugar.

- If a recipe calls for one cup of sugar, substitute 1/2 cup (120 milliliters) honey. Honey is a type of sugar, but it carries more concentrated sweetening power than ordinary table sugar. A tablespoon of ordinary table sugar contains 45 calories. But you need only about 30 calories of honey to get the same sweetening power as provided by 45 calories of table sugar.

- Or in some recipes, substitute 1/2 cup (120 milliliters) molasses for one cup of sugar.

- Sweeten a food such as yogurt with fresh fruits or fruit puree on pancakes and waffles.

- Reduce sugar in a recipe, and add cinnamon and nutmeg. Or use those spices instead of sugar to sweeten a hot drink.

- Make food at home instead of buying prepared foods, with their ubiquitous higher levels of sugar.

The best fats.

Fats are a source of extremely concentrated energy. Their high density of calories can make people fat, especially in the United States, where people tend to take in as much as 40 percent of their food in flavorful, satisfying fat. On the other hand, fat provides energy, even during a time of starvation. Because fat digests very slowly, it makes people feel full and keeps them from feeling hungry. Fat is necessary to cushion some inner organs and skin, especially cushioning against heat loss. The body of even a very thin woman contains a higher proportion of fat than a man's body of the same weight. The woman has unique needs during pregnancy and breastfeeding which make this extra proportion of fat necessary to have.

Besides their role in providing energy, fats provide fatty acids essential to the brain, nervous system, and liver. But, of course, the issue of dietary fat is complicated. For the most part, adults and older children eat too much fat and the wrong types of fat. Yet babies and toddlers, especially, need the good fats. Because of this, the shopper for the family with small children may need to buy a variety of milk, since the restrictions on fat with which most adults live do not apply to milk for small children. Adults and older children need less fat and ought to drink nonfat or low-fat milk. A child under age two ought to drink whole milk.

Here are some of the best sources of fat for a child:

- Mother's milk
- Whole cow's milk and other dairy products after the child is one year old
- Avocados
- A few good cooking oils such as canola, flaxseed, olive, pumpkin seed, or soy bean.

For more about how to buy fats and oils—and which fats and oils to avoid—see Chapter 22, "Fats, Oils, and Spreads."

The best sources of iron.

Iron is essential to carrying oxygen in the blood from the lungs to all the tissues of the body. It's an important element in helping the brain and nervous system to function.

Iron deficiency is the most common form of malnutrition in developed countries, especially among women. Toddlers, infamous for their finicky appetites, often tend toward iron deficiencies. A person with iron-deficiency anemia is not getting enough oxygen throughout the body and is therefore easily tired and worn-out—and with a toddler, probably even more cranky and finicky. Iron deficiency anemia can interfere with development.

Cow's milk is not a good source of iron, which is one reason it's important to keep breastfeeding the older baby since the small amount of iron in human milk is very well absorbed. And it's particularly important to include iron-rich foods (and perhaps an iron supplement) for a growing baby who is ready to have other food besides milk. Serve an iron-rich food along with a food high in vitamin C. That aids absorption.

One reason that iron deficiency has become common is that cooks no longer use iron pots and pans. Cooking in iron helps to add iron to food—safely, too. Here are the best sources of dietary iron:

- Lean meats and poultry
- Organ meats such as beef liver
- Green leafy vegetables
- Wheat germ and whole-grain cereals and flours, especially barley and quinoa
- Egg yolks
- Legumes, including lentils, chickpeas, lima beans, pinto beans
- Fruits such as apricots, bananas, and prunes
- Rice
- Dried fruits and vegetables such as raisins, apricots, and legumes
- Blackstrap molasses
- Tofu and other soy products
- Potatoes

The best sources of calcium.

Nearly all bodily calcium is in bones and teeth. Calcium is essential to the constant rebuilding and replenishing of bones and teeth. Calcium helps the muscles contract, and it is essential to blood clotting. It activates digestion, carries nerve impulses, and performs a variety of critical activities within the body. Here are the best sources of calcium:

- Milk, yogurt, cottage cheese, and other milk products
- Sardines, clams, canned mackerel, canned salmon
- Calcium enriched tofu, soy flour, and other soy products
- Dark leafy green vegetables, although not spinach
- Almonds
- Vegetables such as beans, broccoli, kale, and okra
- Calcium-fortified juices
- Blackstrap molasses

The best sources of fiber.

Fiber provides no calories or nutrients. But it does keep the intestines working well. Toddlers can suffer from problems with elimination, and you may need to make sure that they consume fiber to keep things going smoothly.

Here are the best sources of fiber:

- Whole fresh fruits and vegetables, rather than juices. These are even better served with their peels and skins, once a toddler is old enough to handle these without choking. The best fruits are apples, apricots, pears, avocados, and berries. The best dried fruits are apricots, prunes, and raisins.
- Beans, especially kidney beans, peas, and chickpeas
- Wheat germ and whole grains and cereals, especially oat bran, wheat bran, all-bran, non-degerminated cornmeal, and barley
- Brown rice

The best sources of vitamins.

A child who is getting a variety of foods is receiving an abundance of vitamins. Indeed, you would not want overconsumption of most vitamins or any mega-vitamins for a child. In some cases, however, a child may need vitamins monitored, and perhaps a special food emphasis or a vitamin supplement.

Vitamin A

Vitamin A is the vitamin that facilitates night vision. It has other important functions, including promoting the normal function of mucous membranes, skin ducts, respiratory and digestive systems. Deficiencies are rare among healthy children eating a varied diet.

Some of the best sources of vitamin A are:

- Milk and milk products
- Organ meats such as liver and kidney
- Egg yolk
- Fish oils such as cod liver oil
- Dark green vegetables such as broccoli, cabbage, collards, and spinach
- Yellow-orange vegetables such as carrots, sweet potatoes, and squash
- Fruits such as apricots, cantaloupes, and peaches

Vitamin C

Vitamin C is important with iron-rich foods, since it enhances absorption of iron. Even more important, vitamin C helps to form and maintain connective tissue

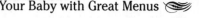

throughout the body. Cooking and processing can destroy vitamin C, so these fruits and vegetables should be eaten with as little processing as possible. Deficiencies are possible, but not likely with any sort of reasonable diet.

Some of the best sources of vitamin C are:

- Citrus fruits such as orange, grapefruit, lemon, and lime
- Other fruits such as melon, pineapple, and strawberries
- Vegetables such as broccoli, cabbage, spinach, and sweet peppers
- Tomatoes

Vitamin D

Vitamin D regulates the absorption and use of calcium and is therefore critical to healthy bones. Generally, deficiencies are only found in people living in extreme northern climates and among heavily clothed children or those who are kept indoors and do not get even a few minutes of sunshine each day.

Some of the best sources of vitamin D are:

- Sunlight
- Fortified milk, yogurt, cottage cheese, and other milk products
- Fish and fish oils such as cod liver oil, herring, mackerel, salmon, sardines, and tuna

You'll see the same important food groups repeated over and over, providing the various types of nourishment that human beings require. The idea is to present your child with a variety of good food choices over time. Your child is on the way to a nourishing, happy, full-strength variety of foods for a lifetime.

Chapter Nine

The Safety Rules

The secrets to keeping food safe enough for a baby are cleanliness and temperature. The overall rule is to keep cold foods cold and hot foods hot. Don't let foods sit around spoiling at room temperature. The other general idea is to keep the whole environment clean whenever a baby is in it.

You can't depend on contaminated food looking or smelling bad enough that you know right away that you ought to get rid of it. Although those are good signs, you will have to be careful about the invisible contaminants. Accidentally carrying contaminants from one place to another is all too easy when you can't see or smell them.

Don't run the risk of contaminants crossing from one place to another:

- Get in the habit of using utensils, when practical, to handle food rather than using your hands.

- Wash your hands after you handle uncooked meats, poultry, seafood, or any other food you believe may harbor bacteria. Wash your hands after you have prepared one type of food before moving on to another.

- Don't just rinse off your hands, either. Let the water get warm, use soap, and wash for at least twenty seconds.

- If you wear plastic gloves to prepare food, wash your hands with the gloves on.

- Keep two colors of kitchen towels. Use one color for drying dishes, and the other color for drying your hands.

- Get kitchen towels into the laundry as often as feasible.

- Sponges take up contaminants easily. Use a paper towel to wipe up spills from animal-based products such as milk, meat, poultry, seafood, and eggs.

- Don't sample a food and then use the same spoon for another purpose. If you want to taste a baby's food, put your own portion aside and taste it with a separate spoon. Leave the baby's portion untouched.

- Clean out your refrigerator regularly, so that drips and drops won't be growing bacteria and contaminating other foods.

- If you defrost meat in the refrigerator, put it on a plate so that juices can't seep onto other parts of the refrigerator and contaminate other foods.

- Rinse fruits and vegetables under running water.

- Wash even produce that you plan to peel. Your knife could carry contaminants through into the edible inside.

- Use a cutting board for food preparation rather than a countertop. You can wash a cutting board better.

- Decide if you prefer a wooden or plastic cutting board. Both are safe, as long as you clean them with hot, soapy water after every use. You can put a small plastic cutting board through a dishwasher.

- Be especially careful to wash a cutting board thoroughly after you use it to work on uncooked meats, poultry, or seafood.

- Wash a cutting board after you have used it to prepare one type of food and are moving on to the next.

- Consider using two cutting boards, one for the meat, poultry, and seafood—and the other for everything else.

- Keep your can opener clean, so it doesn't drop contaminants into cans as you open them.

How to sanitize a cutting board or other kitchen implement:

- Mix one quart (one liter) water with one teaspoon (15 milliliters) chlorine bleach.

- Soak the board or other implement in the solution for a few minutes. If the board is too large for soaking, get it wet with the solution and keep it wet for a few minutes.

- Do not rinse.

- Dry it with paper towels or let it dry in the air.

Keep food and leftovers at temperatures too cold or too hot for bacteria to thrive.

- Deal with leftovers as soon as possible. Wrap them well, and put them in the refrigerator or freezer. There's a Two-Hour Rule. Once a perishable food is left at room temperature for two hours, you should discard it. But with food for a baby, make that one hour or less. Immediate is best.

- Once you open a can, jar, or food package, you can expect a food to begin deteriorating.

- Keep cold food in the refrigerator until you're ready to prepare or serve it.

- Defrost foods only in the refrigerator or microwave. Don't leave them out to thaw at room temperature.

- Store food in cabinets that are not directly next to the stove or dishwasher. Those appliances generate heat.

- When you reheat liquid-based leftovers such as soup, make sure to bring them to a boil. Just warm enough to eat is not warm enough for safety.

- When you heat food in a microwave oven, make sure it is heated all the way through. Stir it, and turn the dish. Otherwise, you'll end up with a cold, or even frozen, spot deep inside.

Keep cold foods cold and hot foods hot.

- Cook foods that are supposed to be hot, especially meats and poultry, to at least 160 degrees Fahrenheit (70 degrees Celsius).

- Reheat leftovers to at least 160 degrees Fahrenheit (70 degrees Celsius).

- Once foods are hot, keep them hot. Ideal is 140 degrees Fahrenheit (60 degrees Celsius) or above.

- Keep foods that are supposed to be cold at 40 degrees Fahrenheit (5 degrees Celsius) or less.

- Keep a refrigerator at 40 degrees Fahrenheit (5 degrees Celsius).

- Keep a freezer at zero degrees Fahrenheit (-18 degrees Celsius).

  Remember that high and low temperatures temporarily stop bacteria from multiplying. But once the food is at room temperature, the bacteria start right in again.

Deal firmly with food safety. This is not a time to be tight-fisted. Sometimes, things have to be wasted.

- If you see mold on food, discard the whole item. Don't just cut around the mold.

- Discard—or avoid buying—produce with cuts, bruises, soft brown spots, wilting, or slime. Get rid of anything that strikes you as the wrong color.

- Don't buy—or discard—cans or jars that are bulging, rusty, stained, or sticky. When you open a car or jar, listen for the lid to pop up as the vacuum seal releases.

- At the store, check the sell-by date. Look for the products with the date farthest away. You may find them in the back of the display.

- The sell-by date is not the same as the use-by date. After the sell-by date passes, you have two more days to use milk and dairy products safely. That's assuming you have kept the foods refrigerated.

- Keep track of use-by dates on products. After the product reaches that date, you must discard it.

- Once it has saliva on it, get rid of it.

- Do not store leftovers in the original container. For example, don't pour leftover milk back into the carton. If you want to keep it, put it into a separate container.

Keep up the discipline in the kitchen.

- Be strict. Children who want to help prepare food must wash their hands first.

- Do not allow sampling of batter with raw eggs in it.

- Do not allow pets into places where you are preparing food. Keep them off countertops and tables.

- After you feed or handle a pet, wash your hands.

Chapter Ten
Not for Baby: Bad, Dangerous & Risky Foods

Parents and caretakers always worry, quite rightly, about babies choking on foods. The best way to prevent trouble is to stay near a baby who is eating. Don't let a baby or toddler run around holding food, cups, bottles, or other objects. And don't let a baby eat while lying down or in the car.

Don't give pieces of food small enough to swallow whole. The worst-case scenario would be slices of hot dog or sausage, just the size to block a windpipe. Give just a small amount of food at a time, so a baby can't cram too much in his mouth at once. Stay away from crunchy, chunky, hard foods until a baby is well over one year old and capable of handling them. Whole raw vegetables and fruits, nutritious as they are, are not safe until well past the first year. For example, if you scrape a spoon along an apple, you get a nice apple shred for a baby, much safer than a chunk of apple.

Be careful even about soft foods. A big glob of bread stuck on the roof of baby's mouth could be unsafe. Do not let a small child have a drink with ice cubes in it. And don't give a child food with a wrapper—or pieces of wrapper—still attached.

Know first aid in case of choking. One action you do not want to take is to ram your hand down a baby's mouth too fast and hard, and thus risk jamming the food down rather than taking it out. Here are foods that particularly present choking hazards for children under one year old—and sometimes beyond:

- Raw, stringy vegetables such as celery sticks
- Carrot sticks cut too thin, or carrot "coins"
- Raw peas, string beans
- Leafy vegetables
- Whole corn kernels, cooked or uncooked
- Whole olives

61

- Whole or unseeded berries, cherries with pits
- Grapes, unless they have been peeled and sliced
- Raisins or other dried fruit
- Chunks of meat, meat with gristle in it, pieces of bacon
- Dry cereal
- Nuts and seeds, including seeds from watermelon or other fruits or vegetables
- Peanuts and peanut butter
- Popcorn

These foods are junk—and also present choking hazards:
- Candies of all sorts, especially hard candies or chewy candy
- Candy bars with nuts in them
- Lollipops
- Chewing gun
- Potato chips, pretzels
- Marshmallows

Some foods are risky for other reasons. Raw eggs can carry salmonella. That's why you should not let a child sample raw dough or batter. Cook eggs until they are not runny. A child does not need "over easy" or soft-poached eggs.

Do what you can to reduce salt in food for babies— and everyone else in the family.

Remember that your baby does not know the taste of salt and does not crave salty food. If you add salt to baby food, you may find it tastes better to you. But the baby will not eat better or find the food tastier whether you add salt or not. Activists had a long hard campaign to convince commercial baby food companies to eliminate extra, added salt from baby foods. Even then, it was there only for the parents who might taste the food and find it too bland. Of course, baby's food ought to be bland, and for anyone old enough, there are seasonings other than salt.

Extra salt can put a strain on a baby's kidneys. Almost even worse, early salt can result in a lifelong craving for high-salt foods and salty snacks. Your child will be assaulted by salt on all sides, in any case, from high-salt fast food to the prepared dinners and lunches marketed specially for children. Since salt is associated with high blood pressure and hypertension in adults, it is well to begin life without added salt.

Your baby will get the dietary minimum of essential salt without additions. Sodium occurs naturally in milk, in many vegetables, in meats, fish, and cheeses.

And despite what you may hear to the contrary, French fries are not counted as a vegetable!

Honey care

In baked goods, honey is a good sugar substitute but do not let a baby have raw honey. Do not coat a pacifier with honey, and do not use it as a spread. The risk is that honey can contain the bacteria that cause infant botulism and affect the nerves and muscles. The same goes for uncooked, unprocessed corn syrup.

Chapter Eleven
Protect Your Baby against Allergies

An allergy is a trigger to the body to react to something as an enemy. A food may cause a reaction in a baby's immune system, so that the baby's body reacts as if the food were a harmful substance. The symptoms can be quite severe and dangerous. Allergies among babies and toddlers are more common than you may think. Allergies cause one out of three of the chronic conditions of childhood.

Intolerance to a particular food is something else. Ordinarily, the symptoms of intolerance are less severe and more temporary than allergies. Still, it can cause trouble for a baby. A nursing mother can sometimes pass on a problem through her milk, even to a food that does not bother her in the least. Usually, that passes by, but it can make for a stressful few hours.

Then there is another category, food addiction. Sometimes, persnickety toddlers get the idea that they want to eat just one sort of food—or else way too much of one food and far too little of the variety of foods that are good for people. The toddler is not really physically intolerant of foods, although that may seem to be the case.

Unfortunately, there is not enough research about childhood allergies, and therefore very little in the way of treatment or cure. The best way to cope is to identify the food that causes the trouble and take it off the menu.

But babies often begin with allergies and then grow out of them. Or they are susceptible to an allergy to food—usually milk—presented too early. But if they get the food later in infancy or childhood, they may never develop the allergy.

How can you tell if your child is particularly susceptible to allergies and food intolerance?

- Other people in the family suffer from allergies or food intolerances.
- Your child suffers from skin rashes.

- Your child suffers from intestinal problems, such as nausea, bloating, gas, or diarrhea.
- Your child suffers from respiratory problems, such as an ongoing runny nose or wheezing.
- Your child seems distressed and cranky.

One problem your baby probably does not have is lactose intolerance. With lactose intolerance, the body lacks an enzyme for digesting the lactose in milk and other dairy products. Since the body cannot digest the lactose properly, the unpleasant result can be cramps, diarrhea, or gas. It's a common problem for adults and older children, but almost unheard of in babies and young children. However, an allergy—or sensitivity—to cow's milk is certainly possible and is sometimes confused with lactose intolerance. That's a major reason babies under one year old should not have cow's milk. Also, a breastfed baby who seems to be lactose intolerant may actually be sensitive to the cow's milk and other dairy products in the mother's diet.

You can avoid allergies and food intolerance.

- If you suspect trouble, keep a food record. You may be able to make a logical connection between a particular food and the reaction.
- If you suspect trouble, watch for a reaction almost immediately or at least within hours. Rarely, symptoms will appear as long as 48 hours after ingestion of the food.
- Delay solid foods until a baby is ready. That way you'll never have to know about some potential allergies and intolerances.
- Don't stop breastfeeding until a baby is ready. That will avoid or at least postpone trouble.
- Introduce a new food gradually. Add to the serving just a bit at a time.
- But keep with a new food. Serve the new food at least twice a week. Repetition gives you an opportunity to observe any allergic reaction. Giving a food over and over in small amounts also allows the baby's body to get used to it. You could be preventing a later, more severe allergic reaction.
- Try different forms of a food and different ways of preparing it. A child who does not tolerate cow's milk may do well with yogurt or a cooked, milk-based pudding or custard.
- Allergy to one food may mean allergy to other foods in the same group. A baby who is allergic to oranges is liable to be allergic to other citrus fruits.
- If a baby is allergic to a food, a nursing mother may have to reduce or eliminate that food from her own diet.

Ways that allergies can complicate your baby's life

- A trace amount of food can trigger an allergy, especially for a small child.
- Commercial foods contain hidden ingredients you could not imagine. A careful reading of the label may help, but even then, some ingredients are hidden under scientific or overly generalized names.
- Commercial foods contain ingredients even the companies don't know. For example, a factory may mass-produce a food, then use the same implements to make another product. Mystery ingredients cross over.
- Allergies to milk, wheat, soy, and eggs are common. Yet nearly every commercial product contains some of those. They're difficult to avoid in processed foods.

Delay the foods most likely to cause allergic reactions and intolerances:

- Beans, other legumes, and peas
- Berries, especially strawberries
- Cabbage
- Chocolate
- Cinnamon
- Citrus fruits and juices
- Coconut
- Corn
- Cow's milk
- Eggs, especially egg whites
- Nuts, especially peanuts
- Onions, especially raw
- Pork
- Shellfish
- Tomatoes
- Wheat

When a baby is ready, begin with foods most likely to be tolerated happily:

- Fruits such as apples, applesauce, apricots, bananas, peaches, pears, plums
- Vegetables such as asparagus, beets, carrots, squash, sweet potatoes
- Rice and grains such as barley, millet, oats

Substitute one ingredient for another.

- In most recipes, you can substitute water for milk.
- In most recipes, you can substitute soy milk for cow's milk.
- You can thicken puddings with cornstarch or tapioca instead of eggs.
- If your baby is allergic to wheat, you can experiment with using flours other than white and whole-wheat. The finished texture will be different, and you don't necessarily use the same amount of flour. For each one cup of flour, you can substitute:

  1. 1/2 cup (120 milliliters) barley flour
  2. 1/2 cup (120 milliliters) rye flour and 1/2 cup (120 milliliters) cornstarch
  3. 1/2 cup (120 milliliters) potato flour and 1/2 cup (120 milliliters) cornstarch
  4. 1/2 cup (120 milliliters) rice flour and 1/2 cup (120 milliliters) cornstarch
  5. 1/2 cup (120 milliliters) rye flour and 1/2 cup (120 milliliters) potato flour
  6. 1 cup (240 milliliters) soy flour and 3/4 cup (180 milliliters) potato flour

Allergy and food intolerance are pervasive problems. Combating them takes dedication and astute observation, but the rewards will be great and immediate.

Chapter Twelve
Feed a Vegetarian Baby

All babies start out as vegetarians. With a good variety of foods, they grow healthy and happy as vegetarians. You do need to plan ahead for a vegetarian diet for a baby. Such a worthwhile endeavor should not be entered lightly.

You will be giving your vegetarian child considerable advantages:

- Your child is less liable to fall prey to the obesity epidemic. Vegetarians are almost never seriously overweight.

- Vegetarians can hope to keep healthy, strong cardiovascular systems. They run less risk than others of colon cancer or gout.

- Vegetarians miss out on the risk of extra contaminants in meat, the higher problems with the E-coli bacteria, and the antibiotics and other drugs that have become routine in the treatment of livestock.

- Your vegetarian child may be prepared for the necessary future. Animal protein is not an efficient source of food. Livestock must consume great amounts of food themselves in relation to the amount of food they will eventually produce. The farmland required to feed one family is considerably less if that family is vegetarian. In times when food is scarce, people have tended to be vegetarians out of necessity. Probably as the world becomes more crowded, and the environment becomes more fragile, greater numbers of people will give up eating meat, at least in large, daily quantities.

- Many people become vegetarians, not out of self-interest, but when they see the cruelties inflicted upon animals in the name of making meat a more efficient and more profitable food.

Vegetarianism has no strict definition. Some people allow themselves fish and chicken but not red meat. Some eat no meat, poultry, or seafood, but do allow milk, dairy products, and eggs. Some emphasize the importance of natural and unprocessed foods. A few impose restrictions so severe that food choices are not easy for them.

If you choose a vegetarian approach, you must be vigilant about your child's food. A child who is growing rapidly and developing in complex patterns can suffer more harm on an unmanaged diet than a full-grown adult. Your vegetarian child must eat a wide variety of foods. The problem is that small children have small stomachs and often very small appetites. A picky eater can present a particular problem to a vegetarian family.

There is no room for junk food in a vegetarian diet for a small child, and very little opportunity for random food selection. Considering the tiny appetite and many nutritional needs of a growing child, it is best to plan frequent small meals, at least four a day. Be careful not to satisfy the small appetite accidentally by giving juice just before meals.

Construct a vegetarian diet.

Human beings and all other living things are built of complex protein. Protein, in turn, is complexly constructed out of amino acids. The body generates most of the amino acids it needs for growth and repair. The other amino acids must come from food.

Meat contains all the amino acids a person needs, since meat comes from another animal of the same basic protein structure. A person who eats meat is getting "complete" protein, a complete setup of all the amino acids that human beings cannot make within their own bodies.

Plants also provide protein, but not all the amino acids in the right pattern and in the right amount. Human chemistry does not coordinate as precisely with plant chemistry as it does with the chemistry of other animals. So plant protein is "incomplete." But it becomes complete in combination with other plant-based foods that mix and match amino acids. These combinations do not need to be eaten at the same meal.

The right combinations are nearly mathematical. Think of food as existing in five groups:

1. Milk and dairy products
2. Grains (cereals, flours, rice, corn)
3. Legumes (beans, peas, and lentils)
4. Seeds and nuts
5. Vegetables (especially the dark green leafy vegetables) and fruits

To make up a complete protein, select food from these groups in patterns:

- Group 1 with group 2
- Group 2 with group 3

- Group 3 with group 4
- Group 4 with group 5

For example, milk and cereal combines groups 1 and 2. A peanut butter sandwich combines groups 2 and 4. Add pea soup with the sandwich, and group 3 comes in.

Some vegetarian main dishes are almost direct substitutes for meat, so that the food groups are combined for a complete protein all—or almost all—in one main dish. Eggplant lasagna, for instance, combines food groups and replicates meat-based lasagna.

The concept of the exact "meat substitute" is really unnecessary to the true vegetarian, who has no desire to think of food in terms of meat substitutes. The commercial meat substitutes may help to begin a new changeover to vegetarian eating. Like the vegetarian hamburger, they may replicate familiar meals. But these meat substitutes are essentially convenience foods and not needed in the long run.

Instead, the vegetarian can think in terms of the best possible sources for the nutritional needs of the human body, especially for children.

The problems with a vegetarian diet are easily avoided, but they do exist.

- To avoid calcium deficiencies, a vegetarian mother would be particularly wise to breastfeed her baby. A common substitute for strict vegetarians is soy formula. Soy formula can keep a baby alive and well, but it is not as good as formula based on cow's milk and certainly not anywhere near as good as human milk. (See page 53 for a list of other calcium-rich foods.)

- After your baby is weaned, consider continuing to give him cow's milk during the early growing years.

- If you do not plan to use cow's milk in the future, get a growing toddler used to soy milk and other soy beverages. Calcium-fortified soy milk is by far the best non-animal source of calcium, although there are others.

- Look for calcium-fortified products such as orange juice and cereals.

- Children usually get sufficient riboflavin (vitamin B_2) from milk and meat. Sources important to vegetarians are rice and whole grains, combined with legumes and dark green leafy vegetables.

- Look for formula or soy beverages fortified with vitamin B_{12}.

- If you are concerned about other vitamin deficiencies that are sometimes possible in a vegetarian (particularly a non-milk) diet, you may wish to provide a toddler with a vitamin supplement. Make sure a child who is not drinking milk fortified with vitamin D gets at least twenty minutes of sunshine every day. Sunlight manufactures vitamin D for the body.

- Find good food sources for iron for virtually every meal. So many children and adults suffer from lack of dietary iron that it is a national problem for both vegetarians and meat-eaters. (See pages 52-53 for a list of iron-rich foods.)

- Along with iron-rich foods, serve foods that aid in the body's absorption of iron. These include fruits and vegetables high in vitamin C. These foods are valuable on their own and, like so many foods, their value is enhanced by the combinations in which one eats them.

- Keep up with research about what is best for a vegetarian child. You may wish to be in touch with a dietitian or a nutritional counselor, as part doing what's best for your child.

What the vegetarian child needs, as a rule, are small servings—but small servings of a wide variety of carefully selected foods. A child may well enjoy foods that offer low nourishment and high calories, but those foods might push aside other foods of higher nutritional value.

You should be prepared that a vegetarian child growing into independence will probably experiment with meat and junk foods. Usually, though, the independent teenager or young adult returns to vegetarianism. Meat and junk don't seem like real sustenance after all.

Your child can grow to be a successful vegetarian for a whole long healthy lifetime—and can come to thank the parents who must work hard to pull it off, even against the pressures of a rare-steak-and-French-fries culture.

Chapter Thirteen
Feed a Finicky, Fussy, Difficult—or Special—Baby

Chances are that you will run into difficulties along the way. Some babies are born with special needs, perhaps because of a medical condition. Some are just difficult for no reason that anyone can discover. Often, these difficult babies grow up to be perfectly delightful, happy, successful people.

One of four children suffers from eating disorders as they grow up—and their parents and caretakers suffer with them. Of children with physical and developmental disabilities, the problems are compounded by eating disorders in one out of three.

Then there is your routine, everyday, run-of-the-mill cranky, demanding, finicky, independence-minded toddler.

Often, the problems begin with colic. Colic is a catch-all term for a baby who cries a lot. Often, the real definition of that diagnosis is that the parents, caregivers, and medical advisers have no idea what's wrong. Colic may be the pain caused by infant digestive problems, especially gastro-esophageal reflux, in which there is a malfunction of the valve-like muscles between the stomach and the esophagus, and acids from the stomach push upward into the esophagus. Or colic may point to a hidden allergy. Babies do outgrow most of these problems.

Here are ways to combat mystery distress:

- Stay observant. Perhaps you can discover something, even something seemingly trivial, in the baby's sustenance or environment that could be causing the trouble.

- A nursing mother should observe what she herself is eating. Perhaps the food she is eating is causing a problem for her baby. If she has changed something in her own diet, that change could be a clue to the mystery.

73

Think particularly about caffeine or mega-vitamin supplements in the mother's diet. If there's a family history of lactose intolerance, and the mother is drinking milk herself, she could be passing on milk proteins to the baby that are causing his fussiness.

- Until you resolve the problem, give your small baby only mother's milk and nothing else. Avoid formula, juice, and even water.

- It is possible for a baby to react even to vitamin drops.

- To help calm your baby (and, if it's the reflux problem, put those stomach acids back where they belong), hold your baby upright against your shoulder or upright in a carrier against your body.

- Arrange a separate, peaceful time to feed the baby. While including your child in family meals may be a good idea in theory, a distressed child may nurse and eat better quietly and apart from other family members.

Sometimes even a very small baby can have psychological problems. Perhaps the baby has been through a traumatic birth experience or needed extensive medical treatment at birth that interfered with early opportunities for bonding with parents. The baby who has been through experiences like that may withdraw from human contact. The distressed infant resists snuggling and even eye contact—and may be too tense to nurse well.

The problem is that then the nursing mother also can become tense. Step back, and really look at your baby. There are people with a strong instinct on what to do for difficult babies. (The latest term is "baby whisperers.") You can teach yourself by looking at your own baby as an individual who is different and unique. You need to approach the baby in an unhurried, unflustered way. Of course, that's easier said than done. Perhaps light massage will help. Perhaps talking softly and pleasantly will help, even when the baby doesn't respond at first. Babies seem to like high-pitched tones, and adults instinctively tend to raise the pitch of their voices when they talk to an infant.

Feed the baby in an unhurried manner, if you possibly can. Take your time, and figure out how to cope with the difficulties.

The more fuss you create yourself, the more you can end up adding to the problem. Babyhood flashes by in what seems like a minute. But the growth and learning that take place are vast and reach throughout a lifetime.

No Food Is Good:

- As a bribe to eat other foods,
- As a reward or as a punishment,
- If the role models don't and won't eat it,
- If there's too much of it to eat,
- If you're expected to eat it when you're not hungry,
- If your parents and caregivers don't want and expect you to grow up to like it.

One common cause of food problems for a growing baby is a too-early introduction of solids. A baby may not be physically able to take in food, chew, and swallow. A child too young to say no to food may nevertheless express displeasure in no uncertain way. The problem in that case is timing. Come back with solids the next day, the next week, or the next month. In the meantime, your child will be developing the ability to eat.

A few children are particularly sensitive to textures. The child will gag (almost deliberately) on lumpy cereal, thick puddings, stringy vegetables. Or the child will reject any food that does not meet a precise standard of crispness.

Here are suggestions on how to prepare food for a sensitive child:

- Make it cold. A time-honored trick that parents and caretakers play is to allow a child to suck on something cold—and then bring on the bitter-tasting medicine. Cold temperatures dull the taste buds, or a toddler may just like milk or other foods better cold.

- Make it warm. Warm milk is often considered soothing and most of us prefer food that is warm.

- Make it sweet. Taste buds change with time but babies and toddlers (and even, it seems, a fetus in the womb) have an instinct for sweet foods. The result is that they can become accustomed to sugar-heavy junk food. If you don't allow junk, they can just as easily become accustomed to other sweet tastes such as applesauce, sweet potato, or orange juice.

- Make it other ways. For example, a child who doesn't like milk may like yogurt, cottage cheese, puddings, and custards. A child who doesn't like vegetables may like vegetable soup. This is a good time to learn to cook.

- Disguise it. Add half a spoonful of wheat germ to enrich cereal. Hide vegetables in with rice, a fruit mix, or soup. This is a good time to be creative.

- Make it to order. Sometimes a finicky child will insist that all foods be mixed together, or all must be entirely separate, maybe even on separate plates. Go right along with these eccentric notions. You and your child will both be happier.

When to worry.

These are the signs of poor nutrition, or possibly of an underlying medical condition:

- Chronic overweight or underweight over time
- Lethargy over time
- Cranky disposition over time

- Hair lacking in luster
- Poor skin tone
- Sleep disturbances
- Frequent respiratory illnesses, wheezing

A healthy child will eventually eat enough to stay alive and well. Of course, you must look out for any hidden illness or developmental problem. But a child who is fussy and difficult about eating does not necessarily have anything the least bit wrong.

An average baby doubles birth weight between four and six months. Then the average baby triples birth weight by one year old. By a second birthday, weight gain has slowed considerably. A two-year-old child will weigh about four times the birth weight. Then it takes two more years, up to the fourth birthday, to gain the birth weight once again.

Obviously, a child must grow more and more slowly as time goes on. In the three-year period from one to four years of age, a child will gain about the same amount of weight as in the first, fast-growing year. So naturally, the appetite must taper off. A growing child just does not need the same number of calories per pound of body weight any more. The natural, in-born instinct is to cut back—and that physical necessity happens just as a toddler begins to explore the world and to become a unique self, independent of parents (and all their annoying opinions about food).

So a finicky, fussy, difficult eater may be all right after all. Sometimes a concerned parent must pretend not to be concerned and allow children to change eating patterns all on their own.

Part Three

Recipes & Food Buying Guide

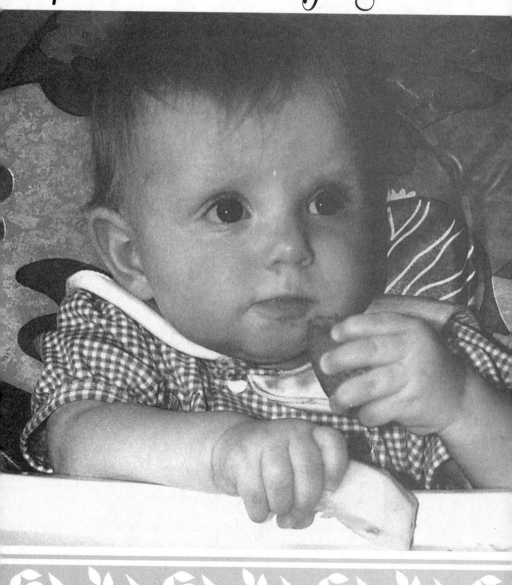

Chapter Fourteen
Cereals

Cereal is often one of the first solids (or semi-solids) babies taste. It can be a nutritious, comforting, everyday food.

But for toddlers, cereals can also become a trap of heavy sweetening, artificial coloring, and empty calories. Some cereals, especially those heavily advertised to children, are the sort of food children can come to crave and demand, but not the sort of food that helps them thrive.

Children and adults need six to eleven servings of carbohydrates a day, in the form of cereals, breads, rice, and pasta. Since that's a major proportion of everyone's food consumption, you'll want to go for the best. You'll want to get your family (and especially your growing baby) in the daily habit of dining on the best, the most delicious, and especially the most nutritious. (Heavily sweetened commercial cereals are not cheap, so going for the best is not necessarily going to cost more.)

One advantage of cereal is that it is unlikely to cause allergies, and it fits in well with a vegetarian diet.

Many nutritionists call for a smooth cooked cereal for a baby's first solid (or semi-solid food). A few feel strongly that brown rice cereal is a better first choice than other sorts of grain. However, if you delay the start of solid foods until a baby is fully ready, no earlier than five or six months of age, any whole grain should be all right.

At first, you may want baby's cereal more liquid than solid. But do not feed cereal in a bottle. A baby who is developing normally and is old enough for cereal and other foods is old enough to learn how to eat from a spoon.

Cereal buying guide.

When you buy cereal, look for a whole grains, natural oats, barley, and brown rice. For a baby just starting, buy a single whole grain, no mixtures or additives. Even for older toddlers who may begin making their own demands, make sure you buy cereals that are enriched and fortified. Do not buy any cereal that contains added sugar or artificial sweetener.

Avoid all brightly colored cereals.

When you buy a cereal that you plan to serve hot, avoid the quick-cooking varieties. Instant cereals often contain extra additives to decrease the cooking time. Yet the time you save is minimal. The preparation time is exactly the same, and the "instant" cooking time saves only a few minutes. Also, many people say that hot cereal cooked slowly, the old-fashioned way, tastes better.

For babies not yet on whole milk, mix cereal with warm water, mother's milk, or formula. The younger the baby, the more liquid you will want to use. By the time your baby is one year or older, assuming there are no signs of milk allergy, you can begin using whole milk.

Make a good cereal better.

Here are ways to enrich cereals, both for nutritional value and for an attractive look and taste:

- Add a sprinkling of wheat germ in cooked cereal or on top of dry cereal.
- Sweeten cooked cereal with pureed fruit.
- Or, for older babies, slice a banana, strawberries, blueberries, or other fruit on top. Take the time. It's worth it.
- Or, for toddlers, mix in raisins, chopped dates, dried banana flakes, or other dried fruit.
- (If you want to make your own granola mix for a toddler breakfast food, see page 168.)

〰Baby's First Cereal, Ground to Perfection〰

Many parents prefer to prepare and cook cereal from natural whole grains rather than to buy a commercial brand. Then they have the option of starting with a single whole grain (usually oats, rice, or wheat), with no additives, and ground to just the right texture. At a health food store, you can buy natural, unprocessed whole grains of oats, wheat, or barley. (The wheat is also called wheat berries or groats.)

For a young baby just starting, begin with an extra fine texture. Within weeks, as baby gets used to eating cereal, you ought to be able to switch to the natural texture, the same as for older children and adults.

Here's one way to create a light, smooth cereal.

Put **1 cup (240 milliliters) whole-grain oats, barley, or wheat berries,** uncooked and dry, into a food processor or blender.

Grind until the grain is as smooth as you want. This takes only five to ten seconds.

You can store the ground oats in a tight container, and use every day. Or you can cook the cereal right away.

〰Baby's First Cereal, Cooked the Old-Fashioned Way〰

Here's how to cook one or two servings of oatmeal. If the baby is just beginning to eat solid food, first grind the oats to an extra-fine texture.

1/3 cup (80 milliliters) rolled oats (1/2 cup or 120 milliliters for older babies, children, and adults)

1 cup (240 millilters) water or milk

In a small pan, combine ground oats with water or milk. If your baby is drinking only bottled or boiled water, then that's the same water you should use to process the oats. Or use mother's milk or formula. Use whole milk only if your baby is past one year old and drinking it without problems.

Cook over moderate heat. Stir occasionally, until the mixture comes to a boil.

Lower the heat, and simmer for a few minutes.

Remove from the heat. Cover the pan, and let it stand for a few minutes.

⌐Baby's First Barley Cereal⌐

Babies are regularly offered barley cereal, while adults hardly ever use this valuable, nutritious grain for their own food. Hulled barley, with only the outer shell removed, is more nutritious than pearl barley, where both the germ and the outer shell have been processed away. The problem is that you may find only pearl barley for sale, and even then you may need to look for it in a specialty natural foods store.

You want to grind your own barley in a food processor or blender. If your baby is just beginning to eat solid foods, grind the barley until it is a fine texture. Store in a tightly sealed container until you are ready to cook it.

Here's how to cook a serving or two for a baby:

3/4 cup (180 milliliters) water or milk (2 cups or 470 milliliters) for older babies, children, and adults)

1/4 cup barley (1 cup for older babies, children, and adults)

In a small pan, bring the water or milk to boil. If your baby is drinking only boiled or bottled water, then that is the same water you should use for this cereal. Or use mother's milk or formula. Use whole milk only if your baby is past one year old and already drinking it without problems.

Sprinkle in the barley, and stir until the water boils again.

Turn the heat to lowest setting, and simmer for a few minutes until the mixture in smooth and creamy. Stir occasionally.

Cover the pan, and let stand for a few more minutes.

⌐Baby's First Wheat Cereal⌐

Here's one way to cook one or two servings of an extra creamy cream-of-wheat cereal.

1 cup (240 milliliters) water or milk

1/4 cup (60 milliliters) whole-wheat cereal (1/2 cup or 120 milliliters for older babies, children, and adults)

In a small pan, bring the water or milk to boil. If your baby is drinking boiled or bottled water, then that is what you should use for this cereal. Or use mother's milk or formula. Do not use whole milk until your baby is one year old and already drinking it without problems.

Sprinkle in the cereal, and stir until the mixture comes to a boil again.

Turn heat to lowest setting, and simmer for just a few minutes until the mixture is smooth and creamy. Stir occasionally.

Remove from heat. Cover the pan, and let it stand for a few more minutes.

⌐Baby's First Cereal, Microwaved⌐

Mix water and oats, barley, or wheat in a microwave-ready container. Then microwave on high setting for 1 to 1 1/2 minutes. Stir. Make sure the cereal is a moderate temperature before you serve it to your baby.

☞Baby's First Cereal, Slow-Cooked☜

If you have busy mornings at your house, you may want to get the cereal started the night before, using a slow cooker.

Mix water and oats, barley, or wheat in a slow cooker.

Cook on the low setting for eight hours, or overnight.

Some people claim that slow cooking produces a particularly delectable taste.

☞A Different Cooked Cereal (for people over nine months old)☜

When your baby is over nine months old, you may wish to use the barley recipe to make bulgur cereal. Bulgur is a cracked wheat good for breakfast cereal and also good for stuffing, salads, and soups. North Americans don't cook with bulgur much, but anyone over nine months of age may grow to enjoy its nutty taste and texture.

☞Baby's First Brown Rice Cereal

Many parents prefer a whole brown rice for a baby's first cereal, rather than a cereal based on wheat or oats. For a baby just starting, you may want a finely ground rice. Put 1 cup (240 milliliters) brown rice, uncooked and dry, in a food processor or blender. Grind until the texture is as fine as you wish. Then you can store it, tightly covered, or cook it right away.

Very soon, you'll find there's no need to grind the rice at all, and you can serve baby the same rice that you cook for the rest of the family.

Here's how to cook one or two servings of brown rice for a baby's cereal.

1/2 cup (120 milliliters) water

2 tablespoons (30 milliliters) fine-ground brown rice

In a small pan, bring water to a boil.

Stir in brown rice. Stir until the water boils again.

Then turn down heat to lowest setting. Cover, and let simmer about 10 minutes or less, until the mixture is thickened.

If your baby is already eating fruit, then soften this with mashed or pureed fruit. If you decide to add more liquid, spoon in a bit of warm water or milk in whatever form your baby already drinks.

〰️Mushy Cornmeal Cereal (for people over nine months old)〰️

Be sure to buy whole—not degerminated—cornmeal. The word "degerminated" makes it sound as if processing has removed nasty germs, but really the word means that the germ, or the heart, of the grain has been removed, along with a good deal of nutritional value. Here's how to prepare four servings of old-fashioned corn mush. Or use it as the basis for little cakes.

You'll need a double boiler.

2 cups (470 milliliters) water

1/2 cup (120 milliliters) whole cornmeal

1/2 cup (120 milliliters) additional water

Additional water

Put two cups (470 milliliters) water into the top of a double boiler. Bring to a boil over direct heat.

In a separate bowl, combine the cornmeal with additional ½ cup (120 milliliters) cold water.

Gradually add this mixture to the boiling water. Cook over direct heat, and stir constantly for several minutes.

Now fill the bottom pan of the double boiler with water, and bring to a boil.

Put the top pan on top, with the water boiling in the pan beneath. Turn down the heat.

Let the mush simmer in the top pan for 15 minutes. Stir frequently.

Serve with milk and fruit. Or make this into baby cakes.

〰️Baby Cakes (for people over one year old)〰️

Here's a way to make cooked cereal into cute little baby cakes that the whole family will like.

Cooked oatmeal, cooked wheat cereal, or corn mush

A beaten egg

Wheat germ

Cooking oil

Roll the cooked cereal or corn mush into a ball. Chill in the refrigerator.

Shape and cut the ball into whatever shapes you like.

Dip your baby cakes into beaten egg. Then sprinkle with wheat germ.

In a medium frying pan, heat cooking oil. Sauté the baby cakes at medium heat until they are browned.

Serve with fruit or cottage cheese.

Chapter Fifteen
Fruits & Fruit Juices

Fruit is of tremendous importance in the diet of a growing child. Fortunately, children tend to like a variety of fruit—and to eat it with enthusiasm and good cheer.

Your time and money are very well spent to provide a selection of fresh, delicious fruit. This is no place to cut too many corners or to worry too much about your convenience. In any case, you rarely need to do a great deal of cooking or elaborate preparation. Usually, all you need to do is to cut up the fruit and remove whatever pits, peels, strings, and seeds may be in the way.

Older children and adults ought to eat three to five servings of fruits and vegetables every day. Nutritionists agree on a few fruits, such as bananas and applesauce, as ideal first foods for babies.

These recommended first fruits are of very low risk for allergy, and good for babies in just about every way. They are:

- Bananas
- Apples and applesauce
- Apricots
- Peaches
- Pears
- Plums
- Avocados

A few fruits are of high risk for allergy, and although they belong in a good diet, you ought to hold off on introducing them until your baby is more than a year old, and is accustomed to a wide variety of foods. These are:

- Citrus fruits such as grapefruit, orange, lemon, and lime
- Berries, particularly strawberries

The only real problem with fruits is that toddlers can fall into a pattern of drinking too much fruit juice, especially highly sweetened commercial juices, so that they don't have an appetite at meals and don't get enough of other nutritious food. Many commercial juices contain too much sugar and very little nutritional value. Occasionally, a baby who drinks too much fruit juice may suffer diarrhea, bloating, and abdominal cramps. So you are wise to limit fruit juices somewhat and not to let a baby drink juice from a bottle or to have juice constantly available. Make sure a baby is used to drinking plain water as an everyday thirst-quencher.

Buying guide for fruits.

If you can buy organic fruit for your baby, you run less risk of hidden fungicides or pesticides. However, organic fruit is almost always more expensive than other fruit, and that is a factor you will have to take into consideration.

When possible, buy fruit that is in season and that has been grown locally. Then you can trust the growing and shipping conditions, at least to some extent. In a global economy, fruit is sometimes imported, and occasionally there have been problems (and very rarely, severe problems) with fruit grown under toxic conditions. So, to be extra cautious with baby's first foods, you may want to buy produce from your own region of the world.

Of course, there are great differences in the prices of fruit. But as you can afford fruits, buy with these preferences, ranging from the highest nutritional (and usually taste) value to the lowest:

- Organic fresh
- Fresh
- Frozen
- Canned in unsweetened juice

You can also save money and avoid some possible toxins if you make it a rule never to buy waxed fruit.

Go for good juices.

When you decide to buy juice instead of making your own, consider these suggestions:

- Make sure that it is 100 percent real juice, unsweetened. Many commercial juices are mostly sugar, corn syrup, and water. Fruit is at best an afterthought. (Remember that in the 1980s, two Beech-Nut executives went to jail for selling apple juice that was plain sugar water, containing no apple at all.)
- Don't buy beverages called "fruit drinks," "fruit cocktails," or "fruit punches." These words are code for artificial sweeteners, coloring, and preservatives—and not much fruit. Buy "natural" juice only if you check the label to make sure just what that word means.

- Look for pasteurized juice.
- Avoid apple juice as more than an occasional drink. It's virtually all carbohydrate.
- Avoid orange juice, grapefruit juice, lemonade, and other citrus juices until your baby is more than one year old.
- Look for juices with some nutritional value, such as red grape, white grape, apricot, and pineapple.
- If the juice looks clear, you could be buying mostly water. Look for a juice you can't see right through, perhaps with some sediment on the bottom.
- Dilute a thick juice with water or, for a treat, carbonated water.
- Once you have opened a juice, store it sealed and refrigerated.

Make a good fruit better.

Here are some ways to reduce risk of toxins (mostly of pesticides and other contaminants) and to enhance nutrition, taste, and convenience.

- Wash fruits thoroughly to get rid of chemical residue. You may want to use a vegetable brush to scrub less delicate fruit. Be particularly careful to wash strawberries, peaches, and cherries thoroughly. You may want to try a commercial additive "wash," specially made to help wash pesticides and even wax off produce.
- Don't use fruits that are moldy, mushy, or cracked.
- Don't add sugar. When your baby is more than one year old, you can add lemon juice to enhance flavor. Lemon juice also helps keep apple slices from oxidizing and turning brown.
- Consider making applesauce or fruit puree in large quantities. Then spoon into ice cube trays. Cover the ice cube tray with plastic wrap. When the fruit is frozen, take out the cubes. Put them into air-tight freezer bags, and then right back into the freezer. Label them with the date, and make sure you use them within three months. To use, just pop out a cube or two, and thaw or heat.
- Serve fruit sauce or fruit puree with mashed banana—or when a baby is ready, sliced bananas and other fruit. Or to serve a high-nutrition meal to an older baby, mix with cottage cheese, yogurt, or soft tofu.

Baby's first banana.

Banana is often the first taste a baby gets of something that isn't milk. Just peel, and pull off the strings. Then cut it up, and mash it with a fork. You don't need a machine, and you certainly don't need a commercial jar, of the sort the advertisers claim is convenient. What's more convenient than a real banana and a fork? Just opening the jar would take you longer than that.

Baby's first apple.

For a first taste of apple, just peel and slice an apple. Then scrape off a bit with the edge of a spoon. The baby can try a few scrapes of apple, and you get to eat the rest.

🍃Baby's First Apricot (or Apple) Sauce🍃

When baby is first eating fruit, you may want to try steaming an apricot or apple, until it is soft and flavorful, good for one or two baby servings. You'll need a steamer basket for this (also useful for fixing tender, nutritious vegetables).

1 cup (240 milliliters) water

1 or 2 apricots or apples

1. Peel, pit, and slice the apricots or apples. Arrange in a steamer basket.

2. In a saucepan, bring the water to a boil. Put the steamer basket into the pan. Cover, and steam about 5 minutes, until soft and tender.

3. Mash with a fork. Or for a baby just getting started, you may to use a blender or a food processor to puree this until it is completely smooth.

Serve warm or cool.

∽Easy Applesauce (Good for the Whole Family)∽

You'll need a food mill for this. But you can prepare lots and lots of applesauce without lots and lots of peeling.

As many apples as you wish

Water

Brown sugar and cinnamon (optional, for older people only)

1. Wash and core the apples, and cut them into sections.

2. Put the apple sections into a large pan, and just cover with water. Boil until they are soft.

3. Carefully spoon these soft apple sections into a food mill. Holding the food mill over a large bowl, crank until the apples come through as applesauce.

4. You may want to put the applesauce through a sieve, or else go through it carefully, to remove any last remaining peels (or the few seeds that sometimes get into the mix).

5. Put the applesauce into a pan, and boil it for one to two minutes. Remove pure applesauce for baby's portion. Then for older people, you may wish to stir in a little brown sugar and cinnamon to taste.

6. Store in refrigerator or freezer. Serve warm or cool.

∽Applesauce, Baked∽

Here's another easy, non-peel way to make applesauce.

1. Preheat the oven to 300 degrees Fahrenheit (150 degrees Celsius).

2. Wash, core, and slice **8 to 10 apples.**

3. Arrange in a large baking dish, and pour in about **1/2 inch (1 or 2 centimeters) water.**

4. Bake for 30 to 40 minutes, until the apples are soft.

5. Spoon these soft apples into a food mill. Holding the food mill over a large bowl, crank until the apples come through as applesauce.

6. You may want to put the applesauce through a sieve, or else go through it carefully, to remove any remaining peel or seeds.

7. Remove pure applesauce for baby's portion. Then, if you wish, add a little brown sugar or cinnamon for older people. Store in refrigerator or freezer. Serve warm or cool.

〰Applesauce, Slow Cooked〰

Here's another easy way to make applesauce—with a slow cooker. You do need to plan ahead.

1. Wash, core, and slice **8 to 10 apples.**

2. Arrange in a slow cooker, and just barely cover with water.

3. Cook on the low setting, for eight hours, or overnight.

4. Spoon these soft apples into a food mill. Holding the food mill over a large bowl, crank until the apples come through as applesauce.

5. You may want to put the applesauce through a sieve, or else go through it carefully, to removing any remaining peel or seeds.

6. Remove pure applesauce for your baby's portion. Then if you wish, stir in a little brown sugar or cinnamon for older people. Store in refrigerator or freezer. Serve warm or cool.

Baby's first avocado.

Avocado is sometimes suggested as a first fruit. You can begin it soon after bananas and apples, or even in place of bananas and apples. Avocados are higher in fat than other fruits, but it's the good kind of monounsaturated fat, just fine for young folk. Avocados are also rich in B vitamins and minerals. Like tomatoes, they are actually a fruit, but are often classified and used as a vegetable.

You can peel an avocado ahead of time, slice in half and cut out the large center pit. Then wrap tightly in plastic, and store in the refrigerator until it ripens. Plan to use it quickly before it gets too soft.

When you want to serve some to baby, just cut off a small piece, and mash it with a fork. Avocados exposed to the air darken quickly. So before you serve avocado to older people, you may want to slow down the oxidizing process by sprinkling it with lemon juice.

Baby's fruit puree.

Ordinarily, all you need is a fork to soften and mash a bit of ripe fruit for a baby. Occasionally, though, you may want to puree fruit with a blender or food processor. First, peel, core, pit, and take out the seeds. Cut the fruit into large chunks. Or use frozen fruits, where all of this is done for you.

You won't need to add water to blend most fruit combinations—or only a very little water.

Then you can experiment with combinations so delicious the whole family will want some. (But since it is wise to introduce all foods to a baby just one at a time, make sure your baby is used to each single fruit before you serve a combination.) Try these fruits pure or combined: apples, apricots, avocados, nectarines, peaches, pears, plums, or strawberries.

For older children and adults, mix the puree with 1/2 to 1 teaspoon (3 to 5 milliliters) lemon juice, 1/2 to 1 teaspoon (3 to 5 milliliters) vanilla extract, or a few drops of almond flavoring. If you wish, top with a few pineapple chunks, grapes, or cherries, cut in half. Serve the fruit sauce by itself or as topping for a frozen dessert.

◆Dried Fruit Strips (for people over one year old)◆

You can make your fruit puree into dried fruit strips. A baby must be at least one year old to eat these.

1. Partially fill a saucepan with fruit puree. **Add 1/2 to 1 teaspoon (3 to 5 milliliters) lemon juice.**

2. Boil and stir occasionally, until the puree thickens to the consistency of molasses.

3. Preheat oven to **300 degrees Fahrenheit (150 degrees Celsius).**

4. Line a baking sheet with foil. Spray with a cooking spray.

5. Spread on the fruit puree.

6. Bake for 20 to 25 minutes.

7. Cool, and wrap in waxed paper. Let dry overnight.

8. Tear or slice into strips.

Apricots make especially good fruit strips.

◆Baby's Broiled Fruit (for people over one year old)◆

For a nutritious dessert the whole family will like, try broiling fruit. Here are a few ideas for broiled, browned fruit desserts.

1. Peel and slice several bananas lengthwise, pears into halves, or a pineapple into strips.

2. Place in a broiling pan.

3. Coat lightly with orange or lemon juice and, if you wish, sprinkle on a bit of brown sugar or cinnamon.

4. Broil for several minutes, until lightly browned.

◆Fresh Citrus Salad (for people over one year old)◆

When your baby is ready for citrus fruit—usually after one year old—cut up segments of grapefruit, orange, and tangerine. Squeeze on juice from the grapefruit and orange. Then top with sliced banana. There's hardly a better taste.

Fruit drinks.

If you own a juicer (even an inexpensive, simple one) or a blender, you can concoct fruit juices that are highly nutritious and highly delicious.

For babies under one year old, try blending a combination of fruits. However, make sure your baby is used to each fruit by itself before you serve a combination juice.

Here are some favorite combinations:

1. Apple juice with banana slices, blended until smooth

2. Apricot juice with banana slices, blended until smooth

3. Apricot juice with peach chunks, blended until smooth

For people over one year old, you can really be creative. You can juice citrus fruits, combine a variety of fruits, and add dairy products. Use plain, unsweetened nonfat yogurt with these options. Here are some favorite combinations for anyone over one year old:

1. 1 cup (240 milliliters) yogurt, blended with banana slices and 1/2 teaspoon (3 milliliters) vanilla extract.

2. 1 cup (240 milliliters) orange juice, blended with banana slices and 1 teaspoon (5 milliliters) wheat germ.

3. 3/4 cup (180 milliliters) orange juice, blended with 10 or 12 strawberries (fresh or frozen, unsweetened).

4. 1/2 cup (120 milliliters) orange juice, blended with 1/2 cup (120 milliliters) raspberries (fresh or frozen, unsweetened) and banana slices.

5. 1/3 cup (80 milliliters) orange juice, blended with 1/3 cup (80 milliliters) plain unsweetened yogurt and 10 or 12 strawberries (fresh or frozen, unsweetened).

6. 1/3 cup (80 milliliters) dried apricots, soaked and sliced, blended with 1/3 cup (80 milliliters) yogurt, 1/3 cup (80 milliliters) orange juice, and 1 teaspoon (5 milliliters) wheat germ.

7. 1/2 cup (120 milliliters) orange juice, blended with 1/2 cup (120 milliliters) seeded melon or cantaloupe chunks.

8. 1/4 cup (60 milliliters) cranberry juice, 1/4 cup (60 milliliters) white grape juice, 1/4 cup (60 milliliters) pineapple juice, and 1/4 cup (60 milliliters) orange juice, blended with banana slices.

For older children and adults, spark up any of these juices with a half cup (120 milliliters) or so of crushed ice, blended in at the same time you blend the juices. Or make a fizzy drink with a last-minute addition of sparkling seltzer water or club soda.

For other choices, see Smoothies, page 128.

Chapter Sixteen
Vegetables & Vegetable Drinks

As your baby is ready, you'll want to present a full range of vegetables, preferably the same vegetables the rest of the family eats. If the rest of the family is not eating a good variety of vegetables, this is the time to get started and to set a good example. Older children and adults ought to be eating three to five servings of vegetables and fruits every day. Some nutritionists recommend seven to eight servings, more than half a person's daily food intake, with the emphasis on fresh, uncooked vegetables and fruits.

Certainly, vegetables ought to be central to everyone's eating, and most North Americans don't get enough, either in quantity or quality.

The best first vegetables for babies, after they are at least six months old, are:

Sweet potatoes

Winter squash

White potatoes

Peas

Some vegetables are high in nitrates, and although they belong in a good diet, you should avoid them until your baby is at least eight months old and able to digest nitrates adequately. These are:

Beets

Carrots

Collard greens

Green beans

Summer squash

Turnips

Spinach

A few vegetables are of medium or high risk for allergies, and although they belong in a good diet, you ought to hold off introducing them until your baby is about a year old, and is accustomed to a wide variety of foods. These are:

Beans

Cabbage

Corn

Onions

Tomatoes

The only real problem with vegetables is that toddlers can fall into a pattern of not liking them, especially those with a strong taste or a texture that a child might find unattractive. Too much vegetable juice can come to replace real vegetables and even to convince babies to resist real vegetables. In any case, a growing baby needs practice with solid food rather than just glugging down juices. So you may want to limit vegetable and fruit juices somewhat. Some parents make it a rule to give no more than four ounces of juice a day.

Sometimes just a different method of cooking or a different way of serving will make vegetables more attractive to children and adults alike.

Buying guide for vegetables.

The ideal is to buy organic produce that is in season and that has been locally grown. Of course, that's not always possible and not always affordable. Frozen vegetables can also be a great convenience. Buy only vegetable drinks that have been pasteurized.

But, as possible, buy with these preferences, ranging from the usually safest and highest nutritional (and most often, taste) values to the lowest:

- Organic fresh
- Fresh
- Frozen, without added sauces

Make a good vegetable better.

- Wash vegetables thoroughly to get rid of chemical residue. Use a vegetable brush to scrub less delicate produce such as celery. You may wish to try one of the new "wash" additives, to make your water more effective in removing pesticides and even wax.
- If you use canned tomatoes or vegetables, buy them without salt or else wash off the salt.
- Consider cooking vegetables in large quantity. Then spoon into ice cube trays. Cover the ice cube tray with plastic wrap. When the vegetables are frozen, take out the cubes. Put them into air-tight, well-sealed freez-

er bags, and then right back in the freezer. Label them with the date and make sure you use them within three months. To use, just pop out a cube or two. Thaw and heat.

- If you're preparing vegetables for the rest of the family, remove the baby's portion before you add salt, sauce, dressing, or other extras. (For vegetable spreads and dips, see pages 158 and 163.)

☞Baby's First Sweet Potato☜

You'll sometimes hear sweet potatoes called yams, although that's not strictly the right name for them. But they do make a perfect first vegetable for a baby. Here is one way to prepare sweet potatoes.

1. Wash thoroughly, then slice one or more sweet potatoes.

2. Place in a small or medium saucepan, and cover with water.

3. Bring water to boil. Cover pan, and turn down heat. Let simmer for about 15 minutes, until the sweet potatoes are soft and tender. Remove peel.

4. Mash the sweet potato with a fork. Or use a food processor or blender to puree. Add water, just to cover the blades. Process at high speed or "puree" for about 30 seconds. Stop the machine once or twice to scrape the sides. Process until the sweet potato is a smooth texture.

5. Serve warm. Store in refrigerator or freezer.

☞Baby's First Vegetables, Steamed☜

Use a steamer basket to produce tender potatoes, peas, squash, broccoli, or other vegetables.

Water

1/2 cup (120 milliliters) vegetables

3 tablespoons (45 milliliters) additional water

1. Peel and cut up potatoes or squash. If you're using frozen peas, separate them with a fork. Arrange in a steamer basket.

2. Fill a pan with about one inch (2 or 3 centimeters) of water, and bring the water to a boil.

3. Place the steamer basket into the pan. Cover, and turn down heat. Let steam for five to ten minutes, until soft and tender.

4. Mash potato or squash with a fork. Or use a food processor or blender to puree peas, broccoli, potato, or squash. Add the water, and process at high speed or "puree" for 60 to 90 seconds. You will need to stop the machine once or twice to scrape the sides. Process until the vegetable is a smooth texture.

5. Serve warm. Store in refrigerator or freezer.

6. For older children and adults, serve with butter. Or make a glaze by melting 2 tablespoons (30 milliliters) butter in a small saucepan. Stir in 1/2 cup (120 milliliters) brown sugar, and 2 tablespoons (30 milliliters) orange juice. Stir and cook until the sugar is dissolved, then boil for one additional minute. Add sweet potato to glaze, and toss gently until well coated.

～Baby's First Baked Potato～

You can bake a sweet potato or white potato just for baby. Just scrub and remove blemishes. Puncture or cut off one end. Then bake at 350 degrees Fahrenheit (180 degrees Celsius) for one hour or more, until the potatoes are soft and tender. Scoop out baby's portion, and make sure there is no peel or blemish. Mash with a fork. Or use a food processor or blender. Add just a bit of water, and process on high or "puree" setting for just a few seconds.

～Baby's First Potato, Microwaved～

You can save cooking time by following the same procedure. Instead of an hour in the oven, though, arrange a sweet potato or potato on a folded paper towel in the microwave oven. Then cook on the high setting for about eight minutes. If you're cooking several potatoes, you may need 12 to 15 minutes.

～Baby's First Potatoes, Slow Cooked～

This way of cooking potatoes takes very little time, but you do have to plan ahead.

1. Scrub as many potatoes as you wish. Cut out blemishes.

2. Wrap each potato in aluminum foil, and place in slow cooker. Do not add water.

3. Or if you wish, peel the potatoes, and add to slow cooker, along with enough water just to cover.

4. Cook on low setting eight to ten hours, or overnight.

5. Scoop out a portion for baby. Make sure there are no peels or blemishes in baby's portion. Mash with a fork.

6. Or if you wish, process baby's portion in a food processor or blender. First, add a bit of water or milk to create a smooth consistency. Make sure the water or milk you add is the kind that your baby already drinks.

7. Serve warm.

～Vegetable Puree～

If you own a food processor or blender, you may prefer to process vegetables such as potatoes, peas, carrots, or beets before cooking. Here's how:

1. Peel, and remove any inedible parts. Cut into chunks or slices, and place in the food processor or blender.

2. For 1/2 up (120 milliliters) vegetables, put in about 1/3 cup (80 milliliters) water.

3. Process on high or "puree" setting for 30 seconds. Stop, and scrape the sides of the machine. Then process for another 30 seconds or less. Keep going until the puree is a smooth texture.

4. In a saucepan, cook at medium heat, and stir, until the puree comes to a boil. Let boil for about one minute.

5. Serve warm. As your baby grows older and is accustomed to a variety of foods, you can try combinations of vegetables and fruits. You can plan to puree vegetables less and less as your baby grows older and is ready to handle food with real texture.

〰Potato and Carrot Puree〰

Here's one way to serve vegetables cooked first and then processed.

1 potato

1 or 2 carrots

Water

1. Peel the potato, and remove the blemishes. Cut into small chunks. Scrape and slice the carrots. Place potato chunks, carrot slices, and water to cover in a small pan. Bring the water to a boil.

2. Reduce heat to low, and simmer, uncovered, about 15 minutes. The potato and carrots should be soft and tender.

3. Cool for a few minutes or longer.

4. Place the potato and carrot pieces into a food processor or blender. Add about 3 tablespoons water or milk.

5. Process at low speed for about 10 seconds.

6. Process at high speed or "puree" for about 30 seconds. Stop the machine once or twice, and scrape the sides.

7. Serve warm. Store in the refrigerator or freezer.

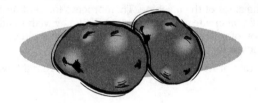

〰Family Mashed Potatoes (for people over one year old)〰

The whole family will consider these mashed potatoes a treat, but serve them only to babies who are drinking and tolerating whole milk.

5 or 6 medium potatoes

Water

1/2 cup (120 milliliters) milk or sour cream

1. Peel the potatoes, and remove blemishes. Cut into chunks. Place in a pan, and cover with water. Bring water to a boil.

2. Reduce heat to low. Cover the pan, and simmer for about 20 minutes, until the potato chunks are tender.

3. Remove the potato chunks to a large bowl, and mash with a fork or a potato masher. If you wish, you can use an electric mixer, food mill, or blender to process them until smooth.

4. Heat the milk or sour cream. (You can do this quickly in a microwave oven.) Mix into the potatoes, until creamy.

5. For older people, you may wish to top with butter. And you may wish to sauté onions in some butter, and add those to the potatoes. Or add chopped parsley.

⤳Peas, Carrots, and Brown Rice⤳

As baby grows older, try a combination of interesting vegetables. This is just one possibility. This recipe allows for leftovers—or for serving to the rest of the family.

2 or 3 large carrots

1 cup (240 milliliters) peas

Water

1 cup (240 milliliters) cooked brown rice

1. Start the brown rice cooking. Or this is a good use for leftover rice.

2. Scrape and slice the carrots. Arrange carrot slices and peas in a steamer basket, and place in a pan with just about one inch (2 or 3 centimeters) of water. Or else place the carrots and peas directly into a medium saucepan, and cover with water.

3. Bring the water to a boil. Then reduce heat to lowest setting, and let steam or simmer for about ten minutes, until soft and tender.

4. If your baby is old enough or if you're serving this to the rest of the family, mix the peas, carrots, and rice. Then serve warm.

5. Or if you wish, use a food processor or blender to puree baby's portion. To process, place the carrots, peas, and rice in the machine, and add ⅛ cup water. Process on high for 30 seconds. Then stop, and scrape the sides of the machine. Then process for another few seconds until you create a smooth texture. You may wish to add another tablespoon of water as you process. As baby grows older, process less and allow for more texture.

6. Refrigerate or freeze the portion you don't serve right away.

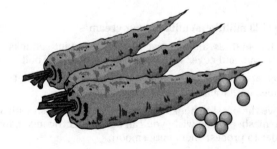

Vegetable Stir-Fry (for people over one year old)

Most older children and adults like stir-fry, so an older baby may go along and make stir-fry vegetables a favorite food. Make sure the baby has been introduced to each vegetable on its own before you try a medley of vegetables. Then you can go for creative combinations. Here's one to try as a colorful family dish. You may want to remove any of the vegetables, such as onion, that you are not sure about for your baby:

2 or 3 carrots

Celery

Red or green pepper, or both

Small onion, optional

Snow peas

Bean sprouts

1/4 cup (60 milliliters) water

1 tablespoon (15 milliliters) cornstarch

1 tablespoon (15 milliliters) soy sauce, if you wish (for people over one year old)

Tomatoes, optional

1. Scrape and cut up the carrots. Wash the other vegetables, and cut up into strips.

2. In a large skillet or wok, melt a small amount of cooking oil or butter. Stir-fry the vegetables at medium-high heat until they are tender-crisp.

3. Combine water with cornstarch. If you are cooking only for older children and adults, also stir in soy sauce. Stir in the combination to thicken the vegetable mix.

4. If you wish, chop one or two tomatoes, and add to the mix. Heat through, and serve warm.

Carrot Salad (for people over one year old)

A finicky child may like grated carrots better than any other kind of vegetable.

2 or 3 carrots

Orange juice

1. Scrape the carrots, and grate with a hand grater or food processor.

2. Moisten with a bit of orange juice.

Vegetable juice.

If you own a juicer, food processor, or heavy-duty blender, you may want to make your own vegetable juice from time to time. You can be creative with vegetable combinations, or here's one suggestion. This is just for one cup, but you may want to double or triple the ingredients for other people to drink.

For other choices, see Fruit Drinks, page 92, and Smoothies, pages 128-129.

> 1/4 cup (60 milliliters) carrot slices
>
> 1/4 cup (60 milliliters) chopped celery
>
> 1/4 cup (60 milliliters) apple, peeled and cut up
>
> 1/4 cup (60 milliliters) apple juice
>
> 1/2 cup (120 milliliters) ice cubes, if you wish

1. Combine in a juicer, food processor, or heavy-duty blender. Process until the mixture is smooth and ready to drink.

2. As a variation—for people over one year old only—substitute pineapple chunks and pineapple juice for the apple.

〰️Tomato Vegetable Juice (for people over one year old)〰️

> A large tomato, peeled and diced
>
> 1/4 cup (60 milliliters) carrot slices
>
> 1/4 cup (60 milliliters) chopped celery
>
> 1/2 cup (120 milliliters) hot water
>
> A few sprigs of parsley, if you wish

1. Combine tomato, carrot slices, chopped celery, and hot water in a juicer, food processor, or heavy-duty blender. Process until the mixture is liquid and ready to drink.

2. Adults may prefer seasoning, such as 1/2 teaspoon (3 milliliters) Worcestershire sauce or 1/4 teaspoon (2 milliliters) Tabasco sauce.

〰️Cucumber Drink (for people over one year old)〰️

> 1/3 cup (80 milliliters) milk
>
> 1/3 cup (80 milliliters) plain, unsweetened nonfat yogurt
>
> 1/3 cup (80 milliliters) cucumber pieces, peeled and with seeds removed

1. Combine milk, yogurt, and cucumber pieces in a blender or food processor. Process on high setting until smooth.

2. For older children and adults, consider adding a bit of crushed ice. Or serve in a frosted glass and garnish with a couple of mint leaves.

Chapter Seventeen
Meats, Poultry & Seafood

You've heard about the Food Pyramid established by the United States Department of Agriculture. The pyramid is designed to give an idea of what foods to eat, in what proportion. High-protein foods such as meat, poultry, fish, and eggs rank at the middle of the pyramid. The USDA recommends two or three servings a day.

The Food Pyramid also ranks some non-animal foods in this category, such as beans and nuts. If you choose a vegetarian menu plan for your child, these proteins can combine with other foods to provide excellent nutrition.

The high-protein, iron-rich foods are important for babies older than eight or nine months. But small servings will do. Your baby—and everyone else—needs high quality rather than great quantity.

Buying guide.

- Buy the leanest meat you can afford. Older babies do need to eat some fat, but not the unhealthful type in red meats.

- Do not buy processed meats for a small child. These include baloney, bacon, ham, hot dogs, pork sausages, and salami. Processed meats are processed with chemicals, and they tend to be high in salt, in nitrates and nitrites, and in unhealthful kinds of fat. In addition, slices of frankfurters or hot dogs are dangerous since they can become stuck in the windpipe of a small child.

- Check the dates on the package, and make sure meat, poultry, and especially seafood look fresh.

- Wait on shellfish and pork. They rank highest in risk to cause allergies in small children.

How to make a good meat better and safer.

- As you prepare poultry for cooking, remove the skin. Trim fat from red meats and poultry. Remove gristle from meats. Remove bones and skin from fish.

- Prepare meats so as to minimize fat. For example, broil meats and poultry in an oven in a grilling pan with a rack, so that the fat drips off into the pan.

- Completely thaw any frozen meat or poultry. Otherwise, it may look well done, but actually have a cold, raw spot in the middle.

- Thaw in the refrigerator or in a microwave oven, rather than on the counter at room temperature.

- Make sure all meat or poultry for children is well done. To be certain, take the temperature of meats, so you can be sure they are cooked adequately. First brown the meat on the outside. Then insert a thermometer. (That way, the thermometer does not carry surface bacteria to the interior of the meat.) The internal temperature should be 165 degrees Fahrenheit (74 degrees Celsius) for most whole and ground meats, and 175 degrees Fahrenheit (79 degrees Celsius) for poultry.

- Fish is cooked thoroughly at the point that it flakes easily with a fork.

- Pre-cooked meats can become contaminated after they leave the factory. Heat, steam, or boil them before serving. Children don't need the poor nutrition of hot dogs, but if you do use them, steam or boil them, too.

- If your favorite recipes have ingredients that are not suitable for children, cook the baby's portion first and remove it before you put in spices, sauces, or other ingredients. Or else serve spices, sauces, and salt at the table, so that older people can add them as they want.

🍞Baby's First Meats, Just the Right Texture🍞

If you're preparing meat, poultry, or seafood for the rest of the family, remove a portion when it is well cooked and before you add other ingredients. Then cut up into small pieces. Use a food processor or blender to prepare. The advantage is that you can begin with a smooth puree, and then proceed to more and more texture, as your baby is ready.

1/2 cup ground or cut-up meat or poultry

2 to 3 tablespoons hot water

1. Process on medium-high speed for about 60 seconds. Then stop the machine, and scrape the sides.

2. As you wish, process again for another 30 seconds, and so on, until the meat is just the right consistency.

Baby's First Chicken, Slow Cooked

One way to make sure your baby's portion is thoroughly cooked is to prepare it in a slow cooker. This is very little work, but you need to plan ahead.

Chicken pieces

Water

Celery, if you wish

Carrots, if you wish

1. Place the chicken pieces in the slow cooker. Cover with water.

2. If you wish, add celery pieces and carrots, scraped and cut up.

3. Cook at low setting eight hours or overnight.

Slow cooking is also a good way to prepare tender, well-cooked chicken for use in chicken salad or other adult dishes. If you can afford it and want to save time, buy boneless chicken breasts.

Big and Little Tuna Loaf (for people over one year old)

If you wish, separate this into a little loaf for your child and a bigger loaf for the rest of the family.

1 beaten egg or egg yolk

1/2 cup (120 milliliters) milk

2 cans (seven-ounce or 196 grams) water-packed white tuna or 1 can (one-pound or .45 kilogram) salmon

1 cup (240 milliliters) bread crumbs

1/2 cup (120 milliliters) chopped onion, for the larger loaf only

1 tablespoon (15 milliliters) lemon juice, for the larger loaf only

1/2 teaspoon (2 or 3 milliliters) salt, for the larger loaf only

1/2 teaspoon (2 or 3 milliliters) dill weed, for the larger loaf only

1. In a large bowl, combine egg or egg yolk and milk.

2. Then mix in tuna and bread crumbs.

3. If you wish, separate out a small portion for your child. Bake it in a small pan or shaped on a baking sheet.

4. Then for the rest of the loaf, mix in chopped onion, lemon juice, salt, and dill weed. Adults might also like some chopped pimiento or olives. Put this larger loaf into a standard loaf pan, about 4 1/2 x 8 1/2 inches (about 12 x 22 centimeters).

5. Bake at 350 degrees Fahrenheit (180 degrees Celsius). Bake the smaller portion for about 30 minutes and the larger portion for about 60 minutes, or until firm.

🥖Big and Little Meat Loaf (for people over one year old)🥖

If you wish, separate this into a small loaf for your child and a large loaf for the rest of the family.

2/3 cup (160 milliliters) bread crumbs

1 cup (240 milliliters) milk

1 1/2 pounds (0.68 kilograms) lean ground beef

2 beaten eggs

1/4 cup (60 milliliters) chopped onion, for the larger loaf only

1 teaspoon (5 milliliters) lemon juice, for the larger loaf only

1/2 teaspoon (2 or 3 milliliters) salt, for the larger loaf only

1/2 teaspoon (2 milliliters) sage, for the larger loaf only

Dash of pepper, for the larger loaf only

1. In a large bowl, combine bread crumbs and milk. Add ground beef and eggs.

2. If you wish, separate out a small portion for your child. Bake it in a small pan or shaped on a baking sheet.

3. Then for the rest of the loaf, mix in chopped onion, lemon juice, salt, sage, and pepper.

4. Put this larger loaf into a loaf pan, about 4 1/2 x 8 1/2 inches (about 12 x 22 centimeters).

5. Bake at 350 degrees Fahrenheit (180 degrees Celsius). Bake the smaller portion for about 30 minutes. Bake the larger portion for about 50 minutes, or until firm.

6. For older children and adults, you may wish to serve the meat loaf with a sauce. Combine 3 tablespoons (45 milliliters) brown sugar, 1/4 cup (60 milliliters) catsup, ¼ teaspoon (2 milliliters) nutmeg, and 1 teaspoon (5 milliliters) dry mustard.

⦃Chicken-Vegetable Timbales (for people over one year old)⦃

A timbale is a sort of custard. Toddlers find it attractive because of its smooth, firm texture, and because it comes in individual servings, just the right size. You may like it because it's an excellent way to use up leftovers. For this recipe, you'll need six custard cups, ramekins, or muffin tins.

1 1/2 cups (360 milliliters) warm milk

1 cup (240 milliliters) chicken stock or broth

Cooked chicken or vegetables

4 eggs, beaten

1. Heat the milk for one minute on the high setting of a microwave oven.

2. If you don't have chicken stock on hand, you can make a quick chicken broth with one cup (240 milliliters) water and two chicken bouillon cubes. Heat this mix on the high setting of a microwave oven for two minutes, until the cubes dissolve.

3. You can use cooked chicken or vegetables, or a combination. Cut up into small pieces. Or else use a food processor or blender to process until smooth.

4. In a large bowl, combine milk, chicken stock or broth, chicken and vegetable, and eggs. Beat with a spoon or whisk until they are thoroughly combined.

5. Butter or oil the custard cups or muffin tins. Pour the timbale mix into the molds, no more than 2/3 full.

6. These molds must cook set in a pan of hot water in the oven. Or, if you prefer, set them on a rack above a pan of hot water. Preheat the oven to 325 degrees Fahrenheit (165 degrees Celsius). While the oven is heating, put in the pan of water to get hot.

7. Set the molds into the pan of hot water. Bake for 20 minutes, or until set. Insert a knife blade, and see if it comes out clean. If not, bake for another 10 minutes.

8. You can serve this in a custard cup or ramekin, or else invert onto a plate. Adults may like paprika or pepper sprinkled on theirs.

Chapter Eighteen

Eggs

Eggs are dense with nutrients. You may be all too familiar with the busy toddler who hardly takes time to eat. Eggs can provide a lot of nutrients in just a few bites.

Eggs contain the highest quality protein. Eggs belong with meats, poultry, seafood, and beans as protein providers, with a recommended two to three servings a day. Almost even better, new studies show that egg yolks contain nutrients that can enhance memory and thought processes throughout life. Some medical researchers say that a woman who eats eggs while she is pregnant enhances the memory capabilities of her baby, even before the baby is born.

Looking ahead to your child's distant future, eggs appear to be a source of nutrients that help prevent age-related macular degeneration of vision.

Nutritionists also like the new specialty eggs that contain higher amounts of vitamin E and more "good" fats than before.

That's the good news. The bad news is that eggs, especially egg whites, are at high risk to cause allergies. So it's wise to wait to introduce egg yolks until your baby is nine or ten months old, and to wait on egg whites until past your baby's first birthday. That also means you must wait on foods that contain eggs. That's difficult sometimes, since foods like custards, cookies, and breads look very attractive to a baby old enough to take notice.

Buying guide for eggs.

- Buy eggs in refrigerated cartons.
- Examine eggs for cracks, and make sure they are not stuck to the carton.
- Don't buy dirty eggs.

Make a good egg better and safer.

- Store eggs in their original cartons, so they stay cool enough. (Those slots for eggs in the doors of some refrigerators keep the eggs too warm.)

- Do not wash the eggs before storing. Washing removes invisible protective coating and could allow bacteria to get into the eggs.

- Wash your hands and cooking tools after you work with raw eggs.

- Cook eggs thoroughly. Do not serve a small child eggs that are soft-boiled, runny, or sunny-side-up.

- Do not use raw eggs in recipes that do not call for cooking. Do not put raw eggs into milk drinks, such as eggnog. (For a way to avoid this problem see Safe Cooked Eggnog, page 129.)

- Do not let a child lick the bowl or eat cookie dough that contains raw eggs (even though television commercials present such extremely informal dining as the way to a happy childhood).

- You can do something to prevent allergies to eggs. For a first introduction to eggs, hard-cook an egg yolk, and begin with a very small amount, just 1/4 to 1/2 teaspoon (2 or 3 milliliters).

- During the time that your baby is eating only egg yolks, you can find good uses for leftover egg whites. Adults who are on a low-cholesterol diet sometimes eat whites without the yolks. Or use whites to replace whole eggs in almost any baked good. You can use up plenty of egg whites in recipes for meringues, angel cake, cake frosting, and white sauces. If you are breading fish or meat, you can easily mix an egg white in place of a whole egg with the bread or cracker crumbs.

🌫Baby's First Hard-Cooked Egg Yolk🌫

Here's how to boil an egg, a traditional skill everyone should have! Boiling the egg makes removing the yolk an easy task.

1. Put the egg (or several eggs) into a small saucepan, and just barely cover with water.

2. To help prevent the shell from breaking, add a dash of vinegar to the water.

3. Bring the water to a boil slowly, over medium heat. Then turn down the heat, and simmer the egg for about 20 minutes.

4. Let cool, or run under cold water to loosen the shell.

5. Peel. Remove the yolk, and mash. You may want to mix the yolk in a soup, or with baby's vegetables.

~Baby's First Poached Egg~

The trouble with boiling an egg is that it isn't really as easy as the proverb says. You can't peer inside to see if the yolk is cooked through. Poach an egg, though, and you can be sure when it's ready.

To poach an egg the old-fashioned way, simmer an inch of water in a small saucepan or skillet. Break the egg onto a saucer. Gently slip it into the simmering water. As the egg cooks, spoon hot water over it to cook the top. Cook five minutes or more, until firm.

If you poach eggs regularly, however, you may want to own a specialty pan with cups that allow eggs to poach over water simmering in the bottom of the pan. Or you may want to try a microwave egg-poaching cup. Either way, poaching baby's egg is faster than boiling, and also produces a good egg, cooked through.

1. Prepare the egg-poaching cup by spraying with a non-stick cooking spray.

2. Break the egg into the cup. Microwave on the high setting for one minute. Or cook over water at medium heat for five minutes. Check to see if the egg is thoroughly cooked. Then you may wish to cook it a bit longer.

3. If your baby is not ready for whole eggs, then remove the yolk and mash.

~Baby's First Scrambled Egg (for people over one year old)~

A baby who is ready for whole eggs will like the taste and texture of scrambled eggs. Older people may like some additions such as a sprinkling of parsley or paprika, a bit of minced onion or chopped green pepper, or grated cheese.

1. In a small bowl, beat an egg or eggs with a fork or a wire whisk.

2. If you wish, add one tablespoon (15 milliliters) milk per egg.

3. Spray a small skillet with cooking spray.

4. Add the eggs, and stir constantly until they are cooked through.

~Toddler's First Omelet (for people over one year old)~

A toddler may be ready for "fancy eggs." Everyone else likes them.

2 eggs

2 tablespoons (30 milliliters) water

1. Separate the egg yolks from the egg whites.

2. In a small bowl, combine the egg yolks with water. Beat with a fork or wire whisk until the yolks are light and foamy.

3. In the small bowl of an electric mixer, beat the egg whites until stiff.

4. Gently fold the whites into the yolks.

5. Spray a small skillet with cooking spray. Cook the egg mixture over medium-low heat, until it is light brown on the bottom.

6. Bake at 325 degrees Fahrenheit (165 degrees Celsius) for five minutes, or until the omelet is set and dry on top.

If you wish, serve with cheese, tomatoes, or vegetables. Adults may like a sprinkling of pepper or chopped parsley.

〜French Toast (for people over one year old)〜

French toast is a favorite among toddlers. Use whole eggs only when your baby is over twelve months old and ready.

1 egg or egg yolk

2 tablespoons (30 milliliters) milk

Slice of bread

1. In a small bowl, combine egg or egg yolk with milk. Beat with a fork or wire whisk.

2. Dip the bread in the egg mixture until it is well coated.

3. On a hot griddle or small skillet, sauté the bread over medium heat, until both sides are browned.

Serve with applesauce or other fruit.

Chapter Nineteen

Soups, Stews, Rice & Pastas

Here are nutritious and delicious ways to prepare full dinners for your baby—and for the rest of the family, too.

Make sure your baby is accustomed to each ingredient before you make a dinner with several ingredients. You don't want a mystery allergy or previously unknown digestive problem appearing.

For a baby just getting started on finger foods, begin with rice pasta. Wait on wheat pastas until you're sure your baby has no problem eating wheat cereals and breads. Unfortunately, the tomatoes and tomato sauce so popular with pastas, stews, and soups, are at high risk to cause allergies. So you'll need to wait until your baby is over one year old before you can serve some family favorites.

Buying guide.

- Buy brown rice from the beginning, and your baby will always prefer its good flavor. Glue-like white rice won't have an appeal.

- You also may want to try millet. Or quinoa is becoming popular as a rice substitute. (That's pronounced "keen-wah.")

- Buy whole-grain pastas and noodles as you can. Appeal to toddlers with fun shapes.

- There are many commercial alternatives to making your own soup stock. But, if you go to the trouble to make your own, you know what's in it. You avoid salt, starchy fillers, and inferior ingredients. You'll be rewarded with superior nutrition—and superior taste, too.

- If you want a good compromise, buy a soup stock, and use fresh ingredients for the rest of your soup. Just check that you're not buying added salt.

- If you don't have the opportunity to make your own soup, buy freshly made soup from a delicatessen. Canned soup, whatever the label says, is all too often salt soup, with an added taste of mush—and the rock bottom nutrition to go with those tastes.

Make a good soup, stew, rice, or pasta better.

- If you plan to make soup or stew regularly, you may want to buy a slow cooker. The advantage is that you don't have to be around to watch it. You can put soup or stew ingredients in the cooker, and let them simmer all day or overnight. You don't need to worry about overcooking or undercooking.

- You may want to establish a routine of making soup stock. The work is not too time-consuming if you make a large amount just once in a while. Then freeze small portions, and use them as liquid when you puree baby food, or as a liquid base for vegetables, meats, soups, stews, and sauces. Pour the stock into ice cube trays, and freeze. Then pop out the individual cubes. Pile them, still frozen, into plastic freezer bags or containers, and put right back in the freezer. These cubes are useful in many ways and certainly better in nutrition and taste than commercial, salted bouillon cubes.

- Use soup stock as pleasant, thin gravy with mashed potatoes or vegetables. Adults may have grown to like the high-fat, high-salt, heavy calories of ordinary gravy, but a bit of this thin stock is much better nutrition, and a small child will most likely enjoy it more than any other kind.

- If you have no soup stock, substitute one cup (240 milliliters) water and two chicken or beef bouillon cubes. Microwave at high setting for two minutes until the cubes dissolve into the water. (Bouillon cubes contain much more salt than soup stock.)

- Brown rice is superior in about every way to plain white rice, but many brands take longer to cook, usually between 45 minutes and an hour. Start the rice immediately, as you think about dinner. By the time you get everything else ready, the rice will be ready, too.

- Here's a handy rule on cooking rice: One cup (240 milliliters) uncooked rice will result in 3 1/2 cups (0.84 liters) cooked rice.

- If you wish to enhance soup or soup stock, as it cooks, put in 2 tablespoons (30 milliliters) pearl barley.

- Add an egg to cream soup, if you wish. In a small bowl, beat the egg lightly with a fork. Then spoon a little of the hot soup into the beaten egg. Stirring constantly, pour this mixture into the soup. That's a procedure to prevent an egg from quick-cooking by accident as it enters the hot soup.

➤Easy, Creamy, Blended Soup (for people who tolerate milk)➤

This is a fast, easy soup, and a good way to use leftovers. You'll need a blender or food processor.

1 1/2 cups (360 milliliters) chicken broth

1 cup (240 milliliters) cooked vegetables, cut up

1/2 cup (120 milliliters) boiled potato, cut up

3/4 cup (180 milliliters) milk

2 tablespoons (30 milliliters) cornstarch or flour, if you wish

1. If you don't have chicken broth on hand, make some by putting three chicken bouillon cubes into 1 1/2 cups (360 milliliters) water. Heat in a microwave oven at the high setting for two minutes, or until the cubes dissolve.

2. Put broth, vegetables, potato, and milk into a blender or food processor. Cover, and blend for about 60 seconds, or until smooth.

3. Pour the soup into a small saucepan. If you wish a thicker consistency to this thin soup, stir in cornstarch or flour. Keep stirring until completely blended.

4. Heat at low setting until warm enough for serving.

5. To serve to adults, sprinkle on salt, pepper, minced onion, and parsley.

➤Lentil Soup, with Vegetable Stock➤

This soup is particularly popular with vegetarian parents.

1 cup (240 milliliters) lentils

3 cups (0.70 liter) water

1 1/2 cups (360 milliliters) vegetable or other soup stock

1 tablespoon (15 milliliters) lemon juice, for people over one year old

1. Use a blender or food processor to blend the lentils and water until smooth.

2. If you wish to use a slow cooker, put in blended lentils, water, and soup stock. Simmer at the low setting for ten hours, or overnight.

3. Or else put the blended lentils and water into a small saucepan, and bring the water to a boil. Cover, and lower the heat. Then simmer for 1 1/2 hours, or until the lentils are tender. Add vegetable or other soup stock, and heat through.

4. For people over one year old, stir in lemon juice. Serve warm.

〰️Pure Vegetable Soup Stock〰️

Make this stock once in a while, and freeze it in small portions, such as in ice cube trays. Then you can use it for a convenient, pure liquid when you prepare other sorts of baby food. You'll need a stockpot, a large soup pan, or a slow cooker.

> 3 large carrots
>
> 2 celery stalks, with leaves
>
> 1 potato
>
> 1 zucchini or other squash
>
> 1/2 cup (120 milliliters) dried white beans
>
> 1 bay leaf
>
> 2 quarts (2 liters) water

1. Scrape and slice the carrots. Wash and slice the celery. Peel and chop potato and squash.

2. In a small skillet, melt a small amount of cooking oil or butter. Over medium-high heat, stir-fry the carrots, celery, potato, and squash, until they are soft and tender.

3. Place the vegetables into a stockpot or slow cooker. Add beans, bay leaf, and water.

4. In a stockpot, simmer about five hours, or all day. In a slow cooker, simmer on the low setting for five hours, or overnight.

5. Put the soup through a sieve or strainer. That removes the vegetables, but leaves in the good nutrition and taste. You end up with pure vegetable broth.

6. If you wish to thicken the broth, stir in 3/4 cup (180 milliliters) milk combined with 3 tablespoons (45 milliliters) cornstarch.

7. Serve this stock on its own, or use it in other soups and dishes. Serve warm.

☞Pure Chicken Soup Stock☜

You can justify the time this takes, since you'll be preparing a number of baby (and family) foods at once. You'll need a stockpot, a large soup pan, or a slow cooker. This makes good, pure chicken stock. Besides the stock, you can also use the chicken and vegetables for a "combination" dinner for your baby. Or else make this stock with white-meat chicken parts, and then prepare chicken salad for older children and adults. This is the exact chicken soup that the mothers of story and legend serve to cure just about anything that ever goes wrong.

About 4 pounds (1.8 kilograms) chicken or chicken parts

3 quarts (3 liters) water

3 large carrots, scraped

3 celery stalks, with leaves

1 onion, chopped

1 bay leaf

Parsley

1. Wash the chicken or chicken parts. Remove any internal organs. Place into the pot, and cover with water.

2. If you are using a stockpot or pan, bring the water to a boil. Skim off any fat that rises to the top. (Some cooks like to skim off the foam, but it contains good nutrient values and does no harm.) Lower heat, and add whole carrots, celery stalks, onion, bay leaf, and parsley bits. Simmer for five hours or more, until the chicken is falling off the bone. You can expect the liquid to be reduced by about a third.

3. If you are using a slow cooker, simmer on the low setting for ten hours, or overnight.

4. Remove the chicken and vegetables. You can cut up chicken meat and vegetables for dinner for an older baby. Or, for a younger baby, use a blender or food processor to puree the tender pieces until smooth. Add a little of the broth as you need to facilitate the processing. Either way, you can freeze this in baby-right portions.

5. Put the soup through a sieve or strainer. You end up with pure chicken broth. If you wish to thicken the broth, stir in 3/4 cup (180 milliliters) milk combined with 3 tablespoons (45 milliliters) cornstarch.

〜Pure Beef Soup Stock〜

This makes good pure beef stock. Besides the stock, you can use it as a whole soup, complete with beef and vegetables. Or you can use the beef and vegetables separately as several dinner portions for baby. This has such a multitude of uses that your time in making it will be very well spent.

You'll need a stockpot, a large soup pan, or a slow cooker.

2 pounds (about 1 kilogram) lean beef

2 large carrots

4 celery stalks, with leaves

3 quarts (3 liters) water

1 bay leaf

1. Cut the beef into small chunks. Scrape and slice the carrots. Wash and slice celery.

2. If you are using a stockpot or pan, bring the water to a boil. Lower heat, and add the beef, carrots, celery, and bay leaf. Cover, and simmer for five hours or more, until the beef is cooked through, and the vegetables are soft and tender.

3. If you are using a slow cooker, simmer on the low setting for ten hours, or overnight.

4. Skim off the fat. Then put the broth through a sieve or strainer. You end up with pure beef stock, useful in many dishes. Save the beef and vegetables for dinner for an older baby. Or for a younger baby, use a blender or food processor to puree the beef and vegetables until smooth. Add a little of the broth as needed to facilitate the processing. However you decide to serve the beef and vegetables, you can always freeze in baby-right portions.

5. An alternative is to serve this as soup for people over one year old. To thicken it, stir in 3/4 cup (180 milliliters) milk combined with 3 tablespoons (45 milliliters) cornstarch. Adults and older children might prefer it with tomatoes and onions cut up into it as it heats and then a sprinkle of parsley on top.

◈Alphabet Soup◈

Make vegetable, chicken, or beef stock fun for toddlers with just a couple of additions.

1. Choose alphabet noodles or other fun noodles or small pasta. Bring a pan of water to a boil, and put in 1/4 cup (60 milliliters) noodles. Boil about five minutes until the noodles are tender.

2. As you heat or reheat stock or other soup for serving, add the noodles. Let them simmer in the rest of the soup for a few minutes.

◈Baby's First Cold Soup (for people over one year old)◈

You'll like this soup, too, on a hot summer day. But your baby may need to get used to different temperatures for foods, as well as different tastes and textures. This is not time-consuming to make, but you'll need to plan ahead, so the soup has several hours in the refrigerator.

4 carrots, scraped and thinly sliced

2 cups (470 milliliters) vegetable or chicken soup stock or broth

3/4 cup (180 milliliters) orange juice

1. Spray a small saucepan or skillet with cooking spray. Sauté the carrots over medium heat until soft.

2. Add soup stock or broth. Cover, and turn the heat to low setting. Simmer for 30 minutes.

3. Use a food processor or blender to puree the mix, about 30 seconds or until smooth.

4. Stir in orange juice. Chill in the refrigerator for two hours or longer.

◈Fish Chowder (for people over one year old)◈

Adults may love clam chowder, but shell fish are of high risk for allergies in babies, so you'll need to wait for clam chowder until baby is fourteen months old or more. Most small children like this mild, creamy soup and enjoy the slightly chunky texture.

1/2 cup (120 milliliters) potatoes, peeled and cut into small chunks

1/4 cup (60 milliliters) carrots, scraped and sliced

1 cup (240 milliliters) vegetable soup stock or broth

1 cup (240 milliliters) cooked haddock or white fish

1/4 cup (60 milliliters) nonfat dry milk powder

1. In a small saucepan, bring the soup stock or broth to a boil. Add the potatoes and carrots. Cover, and turn to low heat. Simmer 15 minutes, or until the vegetables are soft and tender.

2. Stir in the cooked fish.

3. Add the dry milk powder, and stir until smooth. Heat through.

☙Chicken and Rice Stew☙

Make this stew when your baby is able to chew and swallow solids and to enjoy a real texture to food. Or you may wish to consider processing baby's portion in a blender or food processor, until it is smooth or just a bit chunky. You can substitute lean, cooked beef chunks.

1/2 cup (120 milliliters) boneless, cooked chicken breast, cut up

1/2 cup (120 milliliters) carrots, scraped and sliced

2 tablespoons (30 milliliters) uncooked or 1/4 cup (60 milliliters) cooked brown rice

1 cup (240 milliliters) chicken or vegetable soup stock or broth

1. Place chicken, carrots, rice, and stock or broth in a small saucepan. Bring to a boil.

2. Cover, and reduce heat to low setting. Simmer about 30 minutes, or until the carrots are soft and tender and the liquid is absorbed.

Serve as a complete dinner.

☙Complete Dinner Pie☙

If a commercial baby food company made this, they'd call it a combination dinner. You can call it a good way to use up leftovers.

1/2 cup (120 milliliters) leftover, cooked beef, ground beef, chicken, or white fish, chopped

1/2 cup (120 milliliters) leftover, cooked vegetables, such as mixed vegetables, peas, carrots, broccoli, or beans

1 to 2 tablespoons (15 to 30 milliliters) soup stock or broth

1/2 cup (120 milliliters) baked, boiled, or mashed potato

1. Arrange the meat or fish, vegetables, and soup stock or broth in a small ovenproof dish or small casserole dish.

2. If you are using a baked potato, remove the potato from its skin, and cut into small pieces. Add a tablespoon or so of soup stock, broth, or milk. Beat the mix with a fork or a wire whisk. Spread the potato over the "combination" dish.

3. Cover the dish. Bake at 350 degrees Fahrenheit (180 degrees Celsius) for 15 to 20 minutes, until heated through.

☙Brown Rice☙

Begin with one cup (240 milliliters) brown rice, uncooked, and you'll end with 3 1/2 cups (0.84 liter) brown rice, cooked. Since you're cooking for a baby or toddler, don't add the usual butter and salt.

2 1/2 cups (0.60 liter) water

1 cup (240 milliliters) brown rice

1. In a medium pan, bring the water to a boil.

2. Stir in the rice, and bring to a boil again.

3. Cover, and lower the heat to the lowest setting. Cook for about 50 minutes, until the rice has absorbed all the water.

This is ideal rice for a stir-fry dinner, with vegetables and chicken, beef, or shrimp.

∽Baby's First Pasta∾

Begin with 1/4 cup (60 milliliters)—or more—small, whole-grain pasta. You may want to try child-attractive shapes such as bow ties or spirals. Sometimes, you can even buy pasta in holiday shapes, such as pumpkins or Christmas trees.

The ideal is to cook pasta until it is in the Italian phrase, "al dente" ("to the tooth"), when it lightly resists the tooth. It's neither too chewy nor too mushy.

1. In a medium pan, bring water to a boil.

2. Stir in about **1/4 cup (60 milliliters) pasta—or more.** Stir slowly, so that the water continues boiling.

3. Boil for 8 to 10 minutes, until you like the consistency.

4. Drain in a colander or strainer.

Small pastas make a good finger food. Save sauces until your baby is over one year old and ready to eat the usual accompaniments to pasta, such as tomatoes and cheese.

∽Macaroni and Cheese (for people who tolerate milk)∾

This is a childhood favorite food. But wait until your child is happily tolerating dairy products

2 cups (470 milliliters) water

1 cup (240 milliliters) macaroni noodles

½ cup (120 milliliters) milk

½ cup (120 milliliters) grated or sliced mild cheese

1. Bring the water to a boil. Stir in macaroni slowly, so that the water continues to boil.

2. Boil 8 to 10 minutes, or until you consider it done.

3. Drain the macaroni in a colander or strainer.

4. Return the macaroni to the pan. Stir in milk and cheese over low heat, until the cheese is melted and the whole dish is heated through.

Chapter Twenty

Milk, Milk Drinks, Cheese, Puddings & Custards

Of course, you want to make sure your child gets enough milk. That's great if it's mother's milk, and okay if it's commercial formula. But here are reasons to stay away from plain cow's milk until your baby is over one year old. And that's not just because your baby ought to begin learning to drink from a cup about (or before) that time.

You may be surprised to know that most nutritionists recommend introduction of dairy products only after a baby is one year old. Some even put the first milk servings nearer two years old. The main reason is that milk and dairy products are of high risk to cause allergies. About five percent or more of adults in North America suffer from a milk allergy. But perhaps as much as seventy precent of children develop a milk allergy if they start drinking milk before they are one year old. It's an allergy almost all of them will outgrow in the next couple of years, by ages two or three. But meanwhile, it's an allergy with unpleasant symptoms: repeated respiratory illnesses, colds, ear infections, perpetual runny nose, wheezing, and sometimes rashes around the cheeks.

Of course, when your child can tolerate dairy products happily, you'll want to go ahead. Dairy products are a rich source of calcium, protein, and other nutrients. Milk can be an especially good nutritional boost to a child who is a picky eater, or when you otherwise fear your child is not getting as wide a variety of foods as you wish.

The Food Pyramid, created for adults, indicates that two or three servings a day is the ideal amount of dairy products, including milk, yogurt, and cheese.

But if your baby seems not to like milk for a time, pay attention. Perhaps it's the baby's body wisdom.

Meanwhile, you can start yogurt and cottage cheese, perhaps as early as nine months old. Yogurt and cottage cheese are much less allergenic and easier to

121

digest than plain cow's milk. In fact, people often eat yogurt as one way to help heal after an intestinal infection. Or people who have been taking antibiotics often eat yogurt as a way to restore helpful bacteria.

Some parents like to introduce rice milk or soy milk, too, especially if the rest of the family likes them. Here's the order in which you ordinarily ought to consider introducing dairy products:

- Rice or soy milk, if you plan to keep them as regular drinks.

- Yogurt

- Cottage cheese

- Whole milk

- Natural cheeses

- Low-fat or non-fat milk

Buying guide.

- When you buy cottage cheese, buy it plain, without added fruits and vegetables. Then make your own good additions.

- When you buy yogurt, buy it plain. Too many yogurt brands are heavily oversweetened. No one needs the empty calories of the yogurts that are pumped with jams, jellies, and sugars. All too many children overindulge on that sort of food and end up not only developing a sweet tooth but also learning to avoid authentic flavors.

- Avoid "heat-treated" yogurt, and if you can, buy a "natural" yogurt with active cultures.

- When you buy cheese, look for natural hard cheese. Or, as a second choice, buy pasteurized processed cheese. That is not as good as natural cheese either for taste or nutrition. But it is superior to cheese-like products, such as cheese food, cheese spreads, and imitation cheese. More and more, these imitation cheeses are replacing real cheese in commercial and restaurant foods such as pizza and pastas. They tend to contain all the fat of cheese with very little of the nutrition. And the processing adds in a multitude of additives and preservatives, gums, and stabilizers.

- Try adding tofu to your family menus. Tofu is a cheese or curd made from soy milk. It's a bland food, but it blends with other foods and absorbs their flavor. You can use it to replace ricotta or cream cheese. Or firm tofu can be sliced and fried or crumbled and added to salads. Or add frozen soft tofu to milk shakes, as a replacement for ice cream. (Try out Tofu Smoothie, page 129.)

- If you decide you want to make your own yogurt regularly, you may want to buy a yogurt maker. A yogurt maker will provide convenient containers and keep the heat at just the right low temperature. Often, it is sold along with a yogurt starter, just the right sort of yogurt for incubating your own.

Make a good dairy product better.

- To dress up cottage cheese, add applesauce or pieces of fruit, such as apple, banana, pineapple, pear, or peach. Or try cut-up vegetables such as green pepper, celery, carrot, tomato, or cucumber.

- To dress up plain yogurt, add applesauce, fruit puree, or cut-up pieces of fruit, such as banana, strawberries, blueberries, peaches, or apple. Or, for older children, try adding 1/4 teaspoon (2 milliliters) vanilla extract and 1/4 teaspoon (2 milliliters) cinnamon to a cup (240 milliliters) of yogurt. Or add a teaspoon (5 milliliters) of lemon or lime juice.

- To make a pleasantly firm yogurt, mix 1 teaspoon (5 milliliters) unflavored gelatin with 3 tablespoons (45 milliliters) boiling water. Mix to dissolve the gelatin. Cool just a bit, and slowly stir into a cup (240 milliliters) of yogurt.

- To enrich a cup of milk shake, add 1 teaspoon (5 milliliters) wheat germ.

- To add a chocolate-like taste to a cup of milk or milk shake, try 1 teaspoon (5 milliliters) carob powder.

Good uses for yogurt.

- Use in place of mayonnaise. Yogurt is more nutritious than mayonnaise and lower in unhealthful fat and pointless calories.

- Use in place of sour cream, especially in recipes for dips and spreads.

- Use frozen yogurt in place of ice cream. Yogurt makes an especially good ingredient for milk shakes and smoothies.

~Your Own Homemade Yogurt~

Use an electric yogurt maker, with the cups that come with it. Or use an electric fry pan and four small, heat-resistant containers with covers.

4 cups (1 liter) milk

3 tablespoons (45 milliliters) live, active yogurt, sometimes called yogurt starter

1. Warm the milk. Whether you use a microwave oven or a stove, heat the milk at low temperature. Do not let it boil. To be extra careful, check with a kitchen thermometer. The milk should be between 95 degrees and 100 degrees Fahrenheit (between 35 to 38 degrees Celsius).

2. Mix yogurt into the milk, and pour into the four containers.

3. Set the containers into the yogurt maker, and cover them. (Of course, follow the instructions that come with the machine.) Or if you are using an electric pan, set the temperature to 100 degrees Fahrenheit (38 degrees Celsius). (That's often the lowest or even below the lowest marked setting.) Add an inch (3 centimeters) or more of hot water, enough to keep the containers warm, and cover the pan.

4. Let the yogurt warm for about six hours, or overnight. The yogurt is finished when it is thick and creamy. Chill. If you wish, save some of this yogurt to use as a starter for your next batch.

~Your Own Homemade Frozen Yogurt~

Just freeze your own yogurt to a soft mush. Remove from the freezer and beat or blend until smooth. Then freeze again. Scoop this into milk shakes, smoothies, fruit juices, and vegetables drinks. Or mix with mashed or pureed fruit. Then freeze, and serve as a frozen ice-cream-like dessert.

~Yogurt for Fun~

Use small gelatin molds or cookie cutters to create fun shapes for yogurt. Or, for individual servings you can use small custard cups. Before you begin, put the molds into the refrigerator to get cool.

1 cup (240 milliliters) yogurt

1 cup (240 milliliters) fruit puree

1 tablespoon (15 milliliters or one packet) unflavored gelatin

2 tablespoons (30 milliliters) hot water

1. Mix the fruit puree into the yogurt

2. In a separate small dish, bring the water to a boil. (This is a good use for a microwave oven.) Mix in gelatin until it dissolves.

3. Add the gelatin to the yogurt mix.

4. Fill the molds or cups. Or else arrange the cookie cutters on a plate, and fill them.

5. Cool in the refrigerator for at least an hour. To remove the yogurt, hold the molds in a dish of warm water while you count to twenty. Then see if you can slide them out onto a plate. Or just lift the cookie cutters, and you can expect the yogurt to slide out.

☙Your Own Homemade Buttermilk❧

When cream is churned into semisolid lumps of butter, there is a delicious liquid left over, buttermilk. Many people relish the taste, and consider it a delicacy, especially in baked goods. Although buttermilk is not widely popular for pure drinking these days, you can still buy commercial bottles of it.

Or if you want a small amount of buttermilk for a particular recipe, keep a package of prepared dry buttermilk powder in your pantry. Then you can have buttermilk instantly.

If you want to use buttermilk regularly (or to prepare your own cottage cheese), you can begin with commercial buttermilk as a starter to make some fresh buttermilk of your own. Or use this buttermilk as a basis for making your own cottage cheese.

1/2 cup (120 milliliters) buttermilk

1 quart (1 liter) whole or reconstituted dry milk

1. Use a blender to blend the buttermilk and milk. Or else stir or shake in a jar. If you are going on to make cottage cheese, pour into a medium saucepan. Cover the jar or pan.

2. Let stand in a warm place for 8 to 10 hours (or overnight), until the milk is thick and clobbered. Or, if you wish to go on to make your own cottage cheese, let it stand another day or so. (See Your Own Cottage Cheese, below.)

3. Refrigerate. Serve as a special drink. Blend into a smoothie. Or use in recipes calling for buttermilk or sour milk.

☙Your Own Cottage Cheese❧

1 quart (1 liter) buttermilk, commercial or homemade

1/2 cup (120 milliliters) cream or sour cream, if you wish

1. Pour the buttermilk into a pan. Let stand 24 hours or longer, until it forms thick curds. The curds should have begun to break away from the sides of the pan or bowl.

2. Use a spatula or spoon to cut the curds into small squares.

3. Heat over the lowest heat setting. Heat very slowly and stir gently, as the curds continue to separate from the whey. Heat to 120 degrees Fahrenheit (50 degrees Celsius).

4. Line a colander or strainer with cheesecloth or a light kitchen towel. Pour in the cottage cheese, so that the whey drains off. Rinse, and let drain again. At this point, some cooks like to stir in cream or sour cream. Decide if you prefer that taste and texture—or not.

Cottage Cheese for Fun

Your baby probably already likes to play with food, and this way of serving cottage cheese with gelatin is extra fun. You can shape it into individual molds. Or chill it in a rectangular pan, and then cut into serving-size blocks.

1/2 cup (60 milliliters) water

1 tablespoon (15 milliliters or one packet) unflavored gelatin

1 1/4 cups (280 milliliters) fruit juice or fruit puree

1/2 cup (120 milliliters) cottage cheese

1. Heat the water to boiling. This is a good use for a microwave oven.

2. Stir in unflavored gelatin until it dissolves.

3. Cool slightly. Stir in fruit juice or fruit puree. Pour into a mold or pan.

4. Refrigerate for an hour or so until partially set. (The time will vary according to the size of the mold or pan.) Then stir in cottage cheese.

5. Chill again until completely set.

6. As variations, try this gelatin by replacing the cottage cheese with grated carrots, sliced bananas, or cut-up pears, peaches, or apricots.

Your Own Instant Sour Milk

Add one tablespoon (15 milliliters) vinegar or lemon juice to one cup (240 milliliters) milk. Let stand for a few minutes.

Cheese Spread (for people over one year old)

You can make your own superior cheese spread, without all the chemicals and preservatives of commercial cheese spread. With this one, you know what's in it. You don't want to scorch this so prepare it over low heat, or use a double boiler. For other spreads and dips, see pages 156-159.

1/2 cup (120 milliliters) milk

1 egg

3/4 pound (.35 kilogram) Cheddar or other mild cheese

1. In a small saucepan, heat the milk over low heat. Or use a double boiler to heat the milk over hot water. Do not let the milk boil.

2. Beat the egg. Grate the cheese. Add them to the milk, and keep stirring.

3. Cook and stir frequently for ten minutes, until the spread is thick and smooth.

4. Put in a covered jar, and cool in the refrigerator. It will keep for up to a week. Use on crackers, toast, and sandwiches. For a variation, try making it with tomato juice instead of milk. Or for older children and adults, add 1/4 teaspoon (2 milliliters) dry mustard.

Rice and Cheese Dinner (for people over one year old)❧

Make this ahead of time, and then bake it in four or five individual custard cups, ramekins, or other small ovenproof dishes. Then you can freeze the dishes, and get out a convenient one serving to reheat any time you wish. Or else use a regular medium casserole dish.

2 1/4 cup (540 milliliters) water

1 cup (240 milliliters) brown rice or 3 cups (720 milliliters) leftover cooked rice

1/2 cup (120 milliliters) grated Cheddar or other natural cheese

1/4 cup (60 milliliters) chopped green pepper, if you wish

1/2 cup (120 milliliters) chopped fresh or canned tomatoes, if you wish

1. If you are preparing the rice fresh rather than using leftovers, bring the water to a boil in a large saucepan. Slowly, stir in the rice so that the water continues to boil. Lower the heat. Cover the pan, and simmer for 45 to 50 minutes, or until the rice absorbs the water.

2. Stir in grated cheese, and continue to simmer until it melts.

3. If you wish, stir in pieces of green pepper and tomato.

4. Pour into individual custard cups or a larger casserole dish. Bake at 375 degrees Fahrenheit (190 degrees Celsius) for 20 minutes.

❧Ground Beef and Cheese Dinner, with Noodles (for people over one year old)❧

This is another dinner you can make ahead in six or seven individual size serving dishes, such as custard cups or ramekins. Then you can reheat a dish whenever you want, for a convenient one serving. Or use a regular large casserole dish.

Water

2 cups (480 milliliters) egg noodles

1/2 pound (.25 kilogram) lean ground beef

2 cups (480 milliliters) cottage cheese

1/2 cup (120 milliliters) yogurt

1 tablespoon (15 milliliters) chopped green pepper, if you wish

1 cup (240 milliliters) chopped fresh or canned tomatoes, if you wish

1. In a large saucepan, bring water to a boil. Stir in the egg noodles slowly, so that the water continues to boil. Boil for eight to ten minutes, or until the noodles seem the right texture. Drain in a colander or strainer, and cool while you prepare the rest.

2. In a small skillet, brown the ground beef over medium high heat. Pour off the grease.

3. Lower the heat. Add cottage cheese and yogurt. If you wish, stir in pieces of green pepper and tomatoes.

4. In a separate bowl, combine the cottage cheese and yogurt.

5. Layer half the noodles into the bottoms of the individual dishes or the large casserole dish. Then layer on the cheese mixture. Then put in another layer of noodles. Top with the ground beef.

6. Bake at 375 degrees Fahrenheit (190 degrees Celsius) for 20 to 30 minutes.

⇜Smoothies (for people over one year old)⇝

Smoothies are all the fashion these days, and they can add taste and nourishment to anyone's diet. Toddlers especially like these milk shake combinations. Make any of them with a blender or food processor. All of these make about one cup (240 milliliters) or a bit more. You can always double or triple the ingredients, if you need more drinks. To make smoothies more convenient, you may want to keep a package of frozen fruit in the freezer for an instant addition.

For other choices, see Fruit Drinks, page 92, and Vegetable Drinks, page 100.

1. 1/2 cup (120 milliliters) milk, with 1/2 cup (120 milliliters) cut-up fruit pieces such as apricot, banana, peach, or strawberries

2. 1/2 cup (120 milliliters) yogurt or frozen yogurt, 2 tablespoons 30 milliliters) water or juice, with 1/2 cup (120 milliliters) fruit pieces such as apricot, banana, peach, or strawberries.

3. 1/2 cup (120 milliliters) yogurt or frozen yogurt, with 1/4 cup (60 milliliters) orange juice and 1/4 cup (60 milliliters) cut-up strawberries.

4. 1/2 cup (120 milliliters) yogurt or frozen yogurt, with 1/4 cup (60 milliliters) orange juice and 1/4 cup (60 milliliters) cut-up cooked carrots.

5. 1/2 cup (120 milliliters) buttermilk, with 1/2 cup (120 milliliters) cut-up fruit pieces such as apricot, banana, peach, or strawberries

6. 1/2 cup (120 milliliters) milk, with 1/4 cup (60 milliliters) orange juice and ¼ cup (60 milliliters) cut-up cooked carrots.

7. 1/2 cup (120 milliliters) yogurt or frozen yogurt, with 1/4 cup (60 milliliters) banana slices and 1/4 cup (60 milliliters) peanut butter.

8. 1 cup (240 milliliters) milk, with 2 tablespoons (30 milliliters) peanut butter.

You can fix up any milk shake with a scoop of frozen yogurt. Or enrich a cup of milk shake with 1 teaspoon (5 milliliters) wheat germ. Or blend in 1/4 cup (60 milliliters) or less crushed ice. Some people like the taste of an added 1/2 teaspoon (3 milliliters) vanilla extract.

⊛Tofu Smoothie⊛

Tofu is a soft, mild soy product that looks a little like cheese. Even if you don't cook with tofu already, you may have eaten it in a Chinese restaurant or in commercial salad dressing. If your family is vegetarian, you'll especially want to try it. Use a blender to make a cup (240 milliliters)—or more—of this cool drink.

1/3 cup (80 milliliters) soft tofu

1/3 cup (80 milliliters) fruit juice, such as orange, grape, or apple

1/3 cup (80 milliliters) banana slices

2 ice cubes

1. Blend tofu, fruit juice, and banana until smooth.

2. Add ice cubes, and blend again.

⊛Safe Cooked Eggnog (for people over one year old)⊛

People love eggnog, especially during winter holidays. But raw egg is not safe for anyone, and certainly not safe for babies or toddlers. There is too much risk of salmonella contamination. Also, raw egg whites are more liable to cause allergies than are cooked eggs. But this is not a problem when you can mix up eggnog and cook the egg at the same time.

1 cup (240 milliliters) milk

1 egg or egg yolk

1/4 teaspoon (2 milliliters) vanilla extract

1/4 teaspoon (2 milliliters) nutmeg, if you wish

1. In a small saucepan, heat the milk over medium heat to just below the boiling point.

2. In a separate bowl, beat the egg with a wire whisk or a fork.

3. Continue beating constantly, and at the same time add the egg to the hot milk in a slow, steady stream.

4. Remove the mixture from the heat.

5. Chill in the refrigerator. If you wish, add vanilla extract and nutmeg.

6. As a variation, you can add some extras to cold eggnog. Blend in 1/4 cup (60 milliliters) orange juice and 1/4 cup (60 milliliters) cooked carrot slices, until smooth. Or blend in 1/4 cup (60 milliliters) pieces of fruit, such as banana, apricot, peaches, or strawberries.

〰️Old-Fashioned Baked Custard (for people over one year old)〰️

This was probably your grandmother's favorite when she was a baby, or even your great-grandmother's. If you want a modern convenience, use a blender or food processor. Bake this type of custard the traditional way, in individual serving dishes in a pan of hot water.

Water

2 cups (480 milliliters) milk

2 eggs

1/4 cup (60 milliliters) sugar or 2 tablespoons (30 milliliters) honey

1/2 teaspoon (3 milliliters) vanilla extract

1/8 teaspoon (2 milliliter) nutmeg, if you wish

1. Pour water into a rectangular pan or dish. Put it in the oven, and preheat the oven to 325 degrees Fahrenheit (165 degrees Celsius).

2. As the water heats, put milk, eggs, sugar or honey, and vanilla extract in a blender or food processor. Add nutmeg, if you wish. Process until smooth. Or else beat with a wire whisk.

3. Pour the mixture into four or five custard cups, ramekins, or other small ovenproof dishes. Carefully set these, uncovered, into the pan of hot water.

4. Bake for one hour, or until a knife inserted near the edge comes out clean.

5. Be very careful while removing the cups. Let cool briefly, and then refrigerate for several hours before serving.

6. A variation is to stir a few raisins into each custard cup before you bake them. If you wish, serve with pears, melon pieces, or other fruit.

〰️Custard by Microwave (for people over one year old)〰️

You don't need to bake this custard. But you do need to plan ahead so there's time for the custard to chill in the refrigerator.

1 cup (240 milliliters) milk

2 eggs

1 tablespoon (15 milliliters) sugar or 1 teaspoon (5 milliliters) honey

1/2 teaspoon (2 milliliters) vanilla extract

1. Pour the milk into a heat-proof cup, such as a glass measuring cup. Heat in the microwave oven on high power for about 1 1/2 minutes, until just below the boiling point.

2. If you wish, use a blender, food processor, or electric mixer to combine the eggs, sugar or honey, and vanilla extract. Or else put them into a large pan, and beat them with a wire whisk.

3. Gradually pour in the hot milk. Process or beat until all the milk has been assimilated.

4. Pour into three or four custard cups, ramekins, or other small heat-proof dishes.

5. Place the cups, uncovered, into the microwave oven, in a circle. Do not let the cups touch, and leave space between each.

6. Heat on medium power for six to eight minutes.

7. Cool briefly, and then refrigerate for several hours before serving.

‿Oven Rice Pudding (for people over one year old)‿

This pudding needs very little preparation time, plus it's a good use for a small amount of leftover rice. But plan ahead, since baking it takes 2½ hours. Older people tend to prefer the added spices, but you'll have to decide since younger toddlers may not be ready for them.

1/4 cup (60 milliliters) rice, cooked or uncooked

2 cups (480 milliliters) milk

1/4 cup (60 milliliters) molasses

1/4 teaspoon (2 milliliters) cinnamon, if you wish

1/4 teaspoon (2 milliliters) nutmeg, if you wish

1/4 cup (60 milliliters) raisins, if you wish

1. Combine the rice, milk, and molasses in an ovenproof dish. If you wish, stir in cinnamon or raisins.

2. Bake at 325 degrees Fahrenheit (165 degrees Celsius) for 2 1/2 hours. Stir occasionally.

3. Serve warm or cool. Store in the refrigerator.

‿Rice Pudding, Slow Cooked (for people over one year old)‿

This takes more preparation time, plus several hours (or overnight) in a slow cooker. But it's a good way to be ready with half a dozen servings of rice pudding. Decide if your child is ready for the added cinnamon, nutmeg, and raisins. You can leave them out, if you wish.

2 1/4 cups (540 milliliters) water

1 cup (240 milliliters) brown rice

1 1/2 cups (360 milliliters) evaporated milk

2/3 cup (160 milliliters) brown sugar

3 eggs, beaten

1 teaspoon (5 milliliters) vanilla extract

1/2 teaspoon (3 milliliters) nutmeg, if you wish

1/2 teaspoon (3 milliliters) cinnamon, if you wish

1/2 cup (120 milliliters) raisins, if you wish

1. In a medium saucepan, heat the water to boiling. Stir in the rice slowly, so that the water keeps boiling.

2. Turn the heat to low, and cover the pan. Simmer for 45 to 50 minutes, until the rice has absorbed the water.

3. In a slow cooker, combine the rice, milk, eggs, and vanilla extract. If you wish, add nutmeg, cinnamon, and raisins.

4. Cook on the low setting for six hours, or overnight.

5. Serve warm or cool. Store in the refrigerator.

Chapter Twenty-One
The Baby Bakery

Bread and other baked goods tend to be our most frequent and most beloved food. That's good. People need six to eleven servings a day of grains such as bread, cereal, pasta, and rice.

But there's a bad side. Many commercial baked goods are low in quality. They are high in unhealthful fats, sugar, even salt. And they do not carry much nutrition.

If you put in time to bake your own, you'll achieve a vastly superior product. All those servings of bread and other grain-filled products will provide your baby with good nutrition instead of empty calories. Even better, baking your own will help your children to grow up with a taste for good food. They won't have the cravings for sugary baked goods that trouble so many adults. Considering the obesity epidemic, this could be almost as good as guaranteeing your child against future cravings for alcohol or tobacco.

Buying guide.

- Read the labels on flour content. "Enriched" flour sounds good. But it's really just refined white flour, with almost all the nutrients processed out of it, and just a few processed back in. And look for "unbleached" flour. Unbleached flour retains more nutrients than the bleached varieties, and it has not been treated with chemical whitening agents. There is no difference in the taste or texture of the finished product. The only difference you can see is that the unbleached flour looks slightly less white.

- When you can, it's best to buy breads, crackers, and baked desserts that contain whole wheat, whole rye, or oatmeal. That's not easy. But look at the labels that list the ingredients in order of proportion in the **133** product, and try to find baked goods where whole wheat (or rye) flour ranks above white flour. Whole-grain flours retain the germ, bran, and original nutrients. (Most of us are used to white flour, so that whole-grain flours may seem too chewy or tough at first. Yet that texture is all to the good nutritionally. It's fiber, and fiber helps digestion. It's good for chewing, especially when a baby is just developing teeth and gum structures.)

- Avoid bromated flours. Bromating can cause skin reactions in susceptible people, especially small children.

- Buy cornmeal that still has its germ. "Degerminated" means that the germ, the center of the grain, has been removed. You don't want it removed because it's the best part. (But its presence makes the grain subject to spoiling. Germinated flour has a shorter shelf life.)

- Read labels on fat content. Bad fat content is another reason to bake your own. Then you know what sort of fat is in it. (See Fats, Oils, and Spreads, pages 153-159.

- Avoid crackers with more than one gram of saturated fat per one ounce. Read the label to see how much as well as what type you're getting.

- Read the labels on sugar content. Avoiding sugar in commercial baked goods is almost impossible, but you ought to have an idea of how heavily sweetened the product is.

- Read the labels on salt content. Many baked goods contain both too much sugar and too much salt. In crackers, look for less than 240 milligrams sodium/salt per one-ounce serving.

- Don't buy for convenience alone. Preparing cake batter from scratch, for instance, takes 20 minutes. Preparing a commercial cake mix takes 15 minutes. The extra five minutes gives you a cake with better taste, texture, and nutrition. (That's our own time estimate, but we don't take into account how many times the children need your attention during any given number of minutes!)

- Do not buy pancake mix. Your own pancakes require mixing perhaps six ingredients. The mix requires putting together four ingredients. You save hardly a whole minute. And there's always the conclusion, a better product.

- Avoid vegetable-flavored crackers. That's just flavoring, not real vegetables.

- Consider whether you wish to buy a bread machine. Enthusiasts (including us) believe that the bread you prepare and knead by hand tastes better than bread-machine bread. Plus there's the matter of the attractively odd shapes and interesting texture you can produce by hand. Also, you can prepare three (or sometimes) more loaves at once. And, of course, bread machines can take up a lot of kitchen space and can be expensive. On the other hand, a bread machine is convenient

and really does save time. Some chefs use the machine to develop and knead the dough, and then shape the dough by hand. That's an especially convenient way to make buns, rolls, bread sticks, or pizza.

- Consider the loaf pans you buy for bread. Most stores sell standard, medium loaf pans at 9 x 5 inches (23 x 13 centimeters). A better size is 8 1/2 x 4 1/2 inches (22 x 12 centimeters). You'll find the bread rises more attractively in the slightly smaller pan.

Make a good baked good better.

- Try baking with at least some whole wheat or whole rye flour. Get your family used to the more interesting texture and more definite taste. Baked goods do not have to be sugary and bland all the time. If you wish, experiment with mixing two parts white flour with one part whole wheat flour.

- Bake with Cornell Triple-Rich Formula. Add this formula to any recipe for bread, cookies, muffins, or any baked good. In the bottom of each cup (240 milliliters) flour called for in a recipe, add 1 tablespoon (15 milliliters) soy flour, 1 tablespoon (15 milliliters) powdered nonfat dry milk (not the instant crystals), and 1 teaspoon (5 milliliters) wheat germ. Fill the rest of the measure with flour. These enrichments add calcium, iron, protein, and vitamins to baked goods, without appreciably altering taste or texture.

- When you make yeast bread, begin by dissolving the yeast in lukewarm water. If the water is too hot, it could kill the yeast. If it is too cold, it could hold back the rising action. Active yeast dissolved in warm water should look bubbly and puff up a bit in just a few minutes. If it doesn't, discard it, and try again.

- Most bread recipes call for you to dissolve the yeast in water, along with a small amount of sugar or honey to help it rise. That's fine, but you also may wish to try diastatic malt powder. It's even more effective in helping yeast develop well.

- Knead dough for yeast bread with the palms of your hands. Punch, fold, and roll over the dough as it becomes increasingly smooth, more elastic, and less sticky. Most people find this pleasant work. If you are called away, cover the dough with a clean towel. It rises better if it is kept consistently warm.

- Let the dough rise, covered with a clean towel, in a warm place. The ideal temperature is 80 to 85 degrees Fahrenheit (27 to 29 degrees Celsius). You can put the bowl over a pan of hot water. Or put it into an unheated oven, but leave the door open slightly and the light on. The light provides some warmth. Do not put the bowl of dough directly on a hot radiator.

- When you bake a cake, instead of using a special cake flour, which is usually not enriched, use ordinary white flour, but for each cup (240 milliliters), add 2 tablespoons (30 milliliters) cornstarch. That will give the light texture of cake flour. Also, if you want a light cake, be sure to sift the flour once or twice. You can tell the difference in your final product.

- When you bake muffins, enrich them with the addition of some mashed banana or grated carrot.

- Instead of syrup, serve pancakes and waffles with applesauce, cottage cheese, or fruit.

〰️Teething Biscuits (past nine months because of egg yolks)〰️

You can use an electric mixer to make this, if you want, but it's just as easy to mix it by hand. These are flat, dry, and hard biscuits for teething babies, so you don't use the same amount of liquid as you might in other baked goods.

1 egg yolk

2 tablespoons (30 milliliters) honey

2 tablespoons (30 milliliters) molasses

2 tablespoons (30 milliliters) oil

1 teaspoon (15 milliliters) vanilla extract

3/4 cup (180 milliliters) sifted whole wheat flour

1 tablespoon (15 milliliters) soy flour

1 tablespoon (15 milliliters) nonfat dry milk powder

1 teaspoon (5 milliliters) wheat germ

1. In a large bowl, mix together the egg yolk, honey, molasses, oil, and vanilla extract.

2. In a separate measuring cup, mix flour, soy flour, dry milk powder, and wheat germ. Then mix into the egg mixture. The dough will be stiff and somewhat dry.

3. Roll out the dough very thinly. There's no need to be exact, but aim for a thickness of 1/8 to 1/4 inch (1 to 2 millimeters). Cut into baby-finger-length rectangles. Place onto a baking sheet.

4. Bake at 350 degrees Fahrenheit (180 degrees Celsius) for 15 minutes. Cool on a wire rack, and store in a tightly covered container.

〰️Zwieback〰️

Here's another dry, hard bread, good for teething. Begin with whole grain bread.

1. Cut the bread in thin slices, about 1/2 inch (1 or 2 centimeters) thick.

2. Cut each slice into three parts.

3. Bake at 250 degrees Fahrenheit (120 degrees Celsius) for one hour.

☞Baby's First Biscuits (for people who tolerate milk)☜

This is so easy to mix that you don't need to bother with an electric mixer.

2 cups (480 milliliters) sifted whole wheat flour

4 teaspoons (20 milliliters) baking powder

3 tablespoons (45 milliliters) butter

3/4 cup (180 milliliters) milk

1. In a large bowl, combine flour and baking powder.

2. With two forks or a pastry cutter, work in the butter.

3. Stir in milk.

4. Transfer the dough to a floured surface, and knead two or three times. Roll out to about 1/2- to 3/4-inch (13 to 19 millimeters) thickness. Cut with a biscuit cutter or round cookie cutter.

5. Place on a baking sheet or in a round cake pan. If you wish, brush the tops with milk.

6. Bake at 425 degrees Fahrenheit (220 degrees Celsius) for 15 minutes, until brown.

7. A variation is to roll out the dough very thinly and then cut into squares. Bake at 425 degrees Fahrenheit (220 degrees Celsius) for 10 minutes. Either way, try serving warm with applesauce or apple butter.

☞Your Own Home-Baked Crackers (for people who tolerate milk)☜

You can make your own crackers, without salt. These are good for teething, too.

2 1/2 cups (590 milliliters) sifted whole wheat flour

2 tablespoons (30 milliliters) soy flour

2 tablespoons (30 milliliters) nonfat dry milk powder

2 teaspoons (10 milliliters) wheat germ

3 tablespoons (45 milliliters) oil

3 tablespoons (45 milliliters) honey

2/3 cup (160 milliliters) milk

1 teaspoon (5 milliliters) vanilla extract

1. In a large measuring cup, mix and sift the whole wheat with soy flour, milk powder, and wheat germ.

2. In a large bowl or, if you wish, the large bowl of an electric mixer, combine oil, honey, milk, and vanilla extract. Blend in the flour mix.

3. Knead one minute or so, until the dough forms a smooth ball. This is dry dough. You may need to add water or milk a bit at a time to create dough you can knead without letting it get too soft.

4. Transfer to a floured surface. Roll out thinly. Cut into baby-finger-length strips.

5. Bake on a greased baking sheet at 350 degrees Fahrenheit (180 degrees Celsius) for 8 to 10 minutes, or until brown.

6. Cool on a wire rack, and store in a tightly covered container.

〰️Graham Crackers (for people who tolerate milk)〰️

Graham crackers are named for the Reverend Sylvester Graham, who, in the early 1800s, invented a new kind of flour as a highly nutritious alternative to the ordinary white flour of his day. What a shame that commercial graham crackers are now all too often made with all the junk ingredients or other baked goods. You can make your own Graham crackers, far more what Reverend Graham had in mind. He also would have urged you to stay healthy with daily exercise, good foods, and a cheerful disposition. Make these crackers with either graham or whole wheat flour. The two flours are about the same. These are good for teething.

1 cup (240 milliliters) sifted graham or whole wheat flour

1 cup (240 milliliters) sifted unbleached, enriched white flour

1 teaspoon (5 milliliters) baking powder

1/4 cup (60 milliliters or ½ stick) butter

1/4 cup (60 milliliters) honey

1/4 cup (60 milliliters) milk

1. In a large bowl, combine graham flour, white flour, and baking powder.

2. Using two forks or a pastry cutter, work in the butter.

3. Stir in honey and milk.

4. Knead one minute or so, until the dough forms a smooth ball. You may need to add milk, several drops at a time.

5. Transfer to a floured surface. Roll the dough out thinly, about ¼ inch (about 6 millimeters) thick. Cut into squares.

6. Bake on a baking sheet at 400 degrees Fahrenheit (200 degrees Celsius) for about 18 minutes, or until brown.

7. Cool on a wire rack, and store in a tightly covered container.

〰️Oatmeal Crackers〰️

These are good for babies who suffer from allergies, since they contain no wheat, eggs, or milk

5 cups (1.2 liters) rolled oats

1 cup (240 milliliters) water

1/4 cup (60 milliliters) honey

1/2 cup (120 milliliters) oil

1. Use a blender to grind the oats until they are extra fine. Add just a half cup (120 milliliters) or so at a time.

2. In a large bowl, mix the water, honey, and oil. Stir in 4 cups (1 liter) ground oats. This is stiff, dry dough.

3. Flour a work surface with the rest of the ground oats. Knead the dough for less than a minute until you have a smooth ball. Transfer it to your work surface.

4. Roll the dough out thinly, about 1/4 inch (about 6 millimeters). Cut into squares. Prick each square with a fork.

5. Place on a baking sheet. Bake at 350 degrees Fahrenheit (180 degrees Celsius) for about 20 minutes, or until brown.

6. Cool on a wire rack, and store in a tightly covered container.

〰Whole Wheat Bread〰

This recipe makes two good-sized loaves, with wonderful taste and splendid nutritional value. It combines the interesting texture and taste of whole wheat with the light quality that white flour imparts to bread. Do not use an electric mixer. Plan ahead. This is not that much work, but figure in the times for rising and baking, and you'll need half a day, beginning to end.

1 tablespoon (15 milliliters or one packet) active dry yeast

1 teaspoon (5 milliliters) diastatic malt powder or 1 tablespoon (15 milliliters) sugar

1/2 cup (120 milliliters) warm water

1 egg, beaten slightly

1/4 cup (60 milliliters) butter, melted

1/4 cup (60 milliliters) honey or 1/2 cup (120 milliliters) sugar

2 1/2 cups (590 milliliters) additional warm water

1 1/2 teaspoons (8 milliliters) salt

3 1/2 cups (0.80 liters) sifted whole wheat flour

3 1/2 cups (0.80 liters) sifted enriched, unbleached, all-purpose white flour

1/2 cup (120 milliliters) soy flour

1/2 cup (120 milliliters) nonfat dry milk powder

1/2 cup (60 milliliters) wheat germ

1. In a small bowl, stir yeast and malt powder or sugar into warm water, until dissolved.

2. Let this bowl stand in a warm place for a few minutes, while you prepare the rest of the ingredients. If the yeast is good and active, it should turn bubbly and puff up a bit.

3. In a large bowl, combine egg, melted butter, honey or sugar, additional warm water, and salt.

4. Sift together whole wheat flour, white flour, soy flour, milk powder, and wheat germ.

5. Stir the yeast mixture into the large bowl.

6. Then add the flour mixture, and stir until the dough begins to come together.

7. Turn the dough onto a lightly floured surface. Knead until it forms a smooth ball and becomes less sticky.

8. Place in a large greased bowl. (You can use the same one you used to mix.) Cover with a clean kitchen towel, and put into a warm place. Let rise for one hour.

9. Punch down, and let rise for one more hour. You can let it rise longer if that's convenient.

10. Punch down, and return the dough to a floured work surface. Knead for a minute, and shape into three loaves. Cover with a clean kitchen towel, and let sit on the work surface for about ten minutes or less.

11. Transfer the dough to three medium bread pans, greased or oiled. Cover with a clean kitchen towel, and let rise in a warm place for about 45 minutes.

12. You can bake this two ways. Preheat the oven to 350 degrees Fahrenheit (180 degrees Celsius), and bake for 40 minutes. Or do not preheat the oven. Put the pans in the cold oven, and set to 420 degrees Fahrenheit (215 degrees Celsius), and bake for 15 minutes. Then turn the oven temperature to 320 degrees Fahrenheit (160 degrees Celsius), and bake for another 20 minutes.

13. Remove from the pans at once, and cool on a wire rack.

🐚White Bread (for people who tolerate milk)🐚

You can create four good loaves with this recipe, enough to last quite some time (and you can freeze them, if you wish). Plus this is a good enriched bread, with plenty of nutrients and lots of good taste and texture. Plan ahead, so you leave time for the hours of rising and baking.

2 tablespoons (30 milliliters or two packets) active dry yeast

1 teaspoon (5 milliliters) diastatic malt powder or 1 tablespoon (15 milliliters) sugar

1/2 cup (120 milliliters) warm water

1 egg, beaten slightly

1/4 cup (60 milliliters) butter, melted

1/4 cup (60 milliliters) honey or ½ cup (120 milliliters) sugar

2 cups (470 milliliters) warm milk

1 cup (240 milliliters) additional warm water

2 teaspoons (10 milliliters) salt

11 cups (2.5 liters) sifted enriched, unbleached all-purpose flour

1/2 cup (120 milliliters) soy flour

1/2 cup (120 milliliters) nonfat dry milk powder

1/4 cup (60 milliliters) wheat germ

1. In a small bowl, stir yeast and malt powder or sugar into warm water, until dissolved.

2. Let this bowl stand for a few minutes, while you prepare the rest of the ingredients. If the yeast is good and active, it should turn bubbly and puff up a bit.

3. In a large bowl, combine egg, melted butter, honey or sugar, milk, remaining warm water, and salt.

4. Sift together the flour, soy flour, dry milk powder, and wheat germ. (Don't be tempted to skip sifting the flour. You can tell the difference in the finished bread.)

5. Stir the yeast mixture into the large bowl.

6. Then add the flour mixture, and stir until the dough comes together.

7. Turn the dough onto a lightly floured surface. Knead until it forms a smooth ball and becomes less sticky.

8. Place in a large greased bowl. (You can use the same one you used to mix.) Cover with a clean kitchen towel, and put in a warm place. Let rise for one hour.

9. Punch down, and let rise for one more hour. You can let it rise longer, if that's convenient.

10. Punch down, and return the dough to a floured work surface. Knead for a minute, and shape into four loaves. Cover with a clean kitchen towel, and let sit on the work surface for ten minutes or less.

11. Transfer to four medium bread pans, greased or oiled. Cover with a clean kitchen towel, and let rise in a warm place, for about one hour.

12. You can bake this two ways. Preheat the oven to 350 degrees Fahrenheit (180 degrees Celsius), and bake for 40 minutes. Or do not preheat the oven. Put the pans in the cold oven, and set to 400 degrees Fahrenheit (200 degrees Celsius). Bake for 15 minutes. Then lower the oven temperature to 320 degrees Fahrenheit (160 degrees Celsius), and bake for another 25 minutes.

13. Remove from the pans at once, and cool on a wire rack.

≈Rye Bread≈

This makes two good-sized loaves. Many parents of children with allergies particularly like it since it contains no wheat, milk, or eggs.

1 tablespoon (15 milliliters or one packet) active dry yeast

1 teaspoon (5 milliliters) diastatic malt powder or 1 tablespoon (15 milliliters) sugar

1/4 cup (60 milliliters) warm water

2 tablespoons (30 milliliters) butter, melted

2 tablespoons (30 milliliters) honey or light corn syrup

1 cup (240 milliliters) additional warm water

1 1/2 teaspoons (8 milliliters) salt

5 cups (1.2 liter) sifted light rye flour

1. In a small bowl, stir yeast and malt powder or sugar into warm water, until dissolved.

2. Let this bowl stand for a few minutes, while you prepare the rest of the ingredients. The yeast should turn bubbly and puff up.

3. In a large bowl, combine melted butter, honey or corn syrup, additional warm water, and salt.

4. Stir the yeast mixture into the large bowl.

5. Then add the flour, and stir until the dough comes together.

6. Turn the dough onto a lightly floured surface. Knead until it forms a smooth ball and becomes a bit less sticky. This dough is supposed to be sticky, though, so don't work too long.

7. Place in a large greased bowl. (You can use the same one you used to mix the ingredients.) Cover with a clean kitchen towel, and let rise in a warm place for one hour.

8. Punch down, and return the dough to a floured work surface. Knead for a minute, and shape into two loaves. Cover with a clean kitchen towel, and let sit on the work surface for ten minutes or less.

9. Transfer to two medium loaf pans, greased or oiled. Cover with a clean kitchen towel, and let rise in a warm place for about one hour.

10. Bake at 420 degrees Fahrenheit (220 degrees Celsius) for 15 minutes. Then reset the oven to 350 degrees Fahrenheit (180 degrees Celsius), and bake for an additional 25 minutes.

11. Remove from pans at once, and cool on a wire rack.

☙Oatmeal Bread☙

This makes two good-sized loaves. Oatmeal is an excellent dietary fiber, and this bread is a good way to get more oatmeal into your family's diet. You are probably most familiar with rolled oats, and that's fine for this bread. You may, however, want to try steel cut oats. Instead of the flattening that "rolls" the rolled oats, steel-cut oats are cut in half. In this (or almost any) recipe, they taste about the same as rolled oats, but they add an interesting texture, somewhat like cracked wheat.

1 1/2 cups (360 milliliters) boiling water

1 cup (240 milliliters) rolled or steel-cut oats

1/4 cup (60 milliliters or 1/2 stick) butter, melted

1/2 cup (120 milliliters) molasses or honey

2 teaspoons (10 milliliters) salt

1 tablespoon (15 milliliters or one packet) active dry yeast

1 teaspoon (5 milliliters) diastatic malt powder or 1 tablespoon (15 milliliters) sugar

1/2 cup (120 milliliters) warm water

5 cups (1.2 liter) enriched, unbleached all-purpose white flour

2 tablespoons (30 milliliters) soy flour

2 tablespoons (30 milliliters) nonfat dry milk powder

1 tablespoon (15 milliliters) wheat germ

1. Pour the boiling water into a large bowl, and stir in the oats.

2. Add butter, molasses or honey, and salt. Let cool to lukewarm— or room temperature, if it's convenient to let it sit a while longer.

3. In a small bowl, stir yeast and malt powder or sugar into warm water, until dissolved.

4. Let this bowl stand a few minutes. The yeast should turn bubbly and puff up.

5. Sift the flour, soy flour, milk powder, and wheat germ.

6. Stir the yeast mixture into the large bowl.

7. Then add the flour mixture, and stir until the dough comes together.

8. Turn the dough onto a lightly floured work surface. Knead until it forms a smooth ball and becomes less sticky.

9. Place in a large greased bowl. (You can use the same one you used to mix the ingredients.) Cover with a clean kitchen towel, and let rise in a warm place for about one hour.

10. Punch down, and let rise for another 30 minutes.

11. Punch down, and return the dough to a floured work surface. Knead for a minute, and shape into two loaves. Cover with a clean kitchen towel, and let stand on the work surface for a few minutes.

12. Transfer to two medium loaf pans, greased or oiled. Cover with a clean kitchen towel, and let rise in a warm place for about 30 minutes.

13. Preheat the oven to 350 degrees Fahrenheit (180 degrees Celsius), and bake for 40 minutes.

14. Remove from pans at once, and cool on a wire rack.

≈Banana Bread≈

2 or 3 ripe bananas

1/3 cup (80 milliliters) butter

1/3 cup (80 milliliters) honey or 2/3 cup (160 milliliters) sugar

1 beaten egg

1 3/4 cup (320 milliliters) flour

2 teaspoons (10 milliliters) baking powder

1/4 teaspoon (2 milliliters) baking soda

1. Slice the bananas, and mash them with a fork to make 1 cup (240 milliliters) mashed banana.

2. Melt the butter. (This is a good use for a microwave oven.)

3. In a large bowl, combine butter and honey or sugar. Use an electric mixer if you wish. Add the egg.

4. In a measuring cup, combine flour, baking powder, and baking soda.

5. Mix into the large bowl, and then stir in the mashed bananas.

6. Transfer to a medium loaf pan, greased or oiled. Bake at 350 degrees Fahrenheit (180 degrees Celsius) for 45 minutes, or until an inserted knife comes out clean.

7. Remove from pan, and cool on a wire rack.

≈Banana Sticks≈

Here's how to make your banana bread into a good finger and teething food. Use all or just part of your loaf. Slice however much you wish of your baked banana bread into baby-finger-size rectangles. Spread out on a baking sheet. Bake at 150 degrees Fahrenheit (65 degrees Celsius) for 50 to 60 minutes, until dry and crunchy.

❧Corn Muffins (for people who tolerate milk)❧

Commercial muffins often leave you stuck with lots and lots of sugar, and virtually no taste, texture, or nutrients. Homemade muffins can give you plenty of taste, texture, and nutrients, without all that sugar.

These muffins use flour, as well as cornbread, so that they're light in texture.

1 cup (240 milliliters) sifted, unbleached, enriched white flour

1 tablespoon (15 milliliters) baking powder

1 teaspoon (5 milliliters) baking soda

1 cup (240 milliliters) cornmeal

1 tablespoons (15 milliliters) honey or 2 tablespoon (30 milliliters) sugar

1 1/2 cups (360 milliliters) milk

2 eggs

1. In a measuring cup, combine flour, baking powder, baking soda, and cornmeal.

2. In a large bowl, beat the honey or sugar and milk. Do not use an electric mixer.

3. In a separate dish, beat the eggs lightly. Stir into the large bowl.

4. Stir in the dry mixture, just to combine. Do not over mix.

5. Spoon into twelve 2-inch (5-centimeters) muffin cups. Bake at 425 degrees Fahrenheit (220 degrees Celsius) for 20 to 25 minutes.

6. Cool on a wire rack. You can also bake this batter in an 8- by 8-inch (20- x 20-centimeters) square pan, and then cut into squares.

❧Fruit Muffins (for people who tolerate milk)❧

Make the recipe for blueberry muffins, but substitute another fruit. Here are four choices:

1. Slice two or three ripe bananas, and mash with a fork, to make one cup (240 milliliters).

2. Wash and drain cranberries. Then chop to make one cup (240 milliliters). Add an additional tablespoon (15 milliliters) of honey or sugar.

3. Peel and core a large apple. Chop to make about 3/4 cup (about 180 milliliters). Also mix in 1/2 teaspoon (3 milliliters) cinnamon and 1/2 teaspoon (2 milliliters) nutmeg.

4. Stir in one cup (240 milliliters) raisins.

〜Blueberry Muffins (for people who tolerate milk)〜

Don't use an electric mixer to make muffins, and don't over mix. The batter is supposed to be lumpy.

1 1/2 cup (360 milliliters) blueberries

2 cups (470 milliliters) sifted unbleached, enriched white flour

2 teaspoons (30 milliliters) baking powder

1/2cup (120 milliliters) oil

1/2 cup (120 milliliters) honey or 1 cup (240 milliliters) sugar

1/2 cup (120 milliliters) milk

1 teaspoon (15 milliliters) vanilla extract

2 eggs

1. Wash the blueberries in a colander or strainer. Drain, and toss lightly with flour.

2. In a measuring cup, combine flour and baking powder.

3. In a large mixing bowl, stir together oil, honey or sugar, milk, and vanilla extract. Do not use an electric mixer.

4. In a separate dish, beat the eggs lightly. Stir into the large mixing bowl.

5. Stir in the dry mixture, just to combine. Do not over mix.

6. Lightly stir in the blueberries.

7. Pour into twelve two-inch (5-centimeters) muffin cups. Bake at 375 degrees Fahrenheit (190 degrees Celsius) for 30 minutes.

8. Cool on a wire rack.

〜Bran Muffins (for people who tolerate milk)〜

1 cup (240 milliliters) sifted unbleached enriched white flour

1 cup (240 milliliters) bran or raisin bran cereal

4 teaspoons (20 milliliters) baking powder

1/4 cup (60 milliliters) oil

2 tablespoons (30 milliliters) molasses

1 cup (240 milliliters) milk

1 egg

1. In a measuring cup, combine flour, bran or raisin bran, and baking powder.

2. In a large bowl, stir together oil, molasses, and milk. Do not use an electric mixer.

3. In a separate dish, beat the egg lightly. Stir into the large mixing bowl.

4. Stir in the dry mixture, just to combine. Do not over mix.

5. Spoon into twelve two-inch (5 centimeter) muffin cups. Bake at 400 degrees Fahrenheit (200 degrees Celsius) for 20 minutes.

6. Cool on a wire rack.

∞Light Pancakes (for people who tolerate milk)∞

Use a blender or food processor to make these pancakes quickly and easily.

1 cup (240 milliliters) sifted enriched, unbleached all-purpose flour

1 teaspoon (5 milliliters) baking soda

2 tablespoons (30 milliliters) oil

1 egg

1 cup (240 milliliters) yogurt or buttermilk

1. In a measuring cup, combine flour and baking soda.

2. In a blender or large bowl, stir together oil and the flour mix.

3. Lightly beat the egg, and blend in, along with the yogurt or buttermilk.

4. Preheat your griddle until it is hot enough that a drop of water bounces a bit on it. Spoon on the pancake batter. Leave space between pancakes so they can expand. When you see bubbles form and begin to pop, turn the pancakes, and cook the other side, until golden brown.

For a variation, when your batter is already blended, stir in 1/4 cup (60 milliliters) blueberries. Serve warm, and top with applesauce, apple butter, fruit, fruit puree, or cottage cheese.

∞Cottage Cheese Pancakes (for people who tolerate milk)∞

Use a blender or food processor to make these pancakes quickly and easily. These are a good way to add cottage cheese to your child's diet, and many small children especially like the taste.

3 eggs

1 cup (240 milliliters) cottage cheese

1/2 cup (120 milliliters) flour

1. In a large bowl, blender, or food processor, blend together eggs, cottage cheese, and flour.

2. Preheat your griddle until it is hot enough that a drop of water bounces a bit on it. Spoon on the pancake batter. Leave space between the pancakes so they can expand. When you see bubbles form and begin to pop, turn the pancakes, and cook the other side, until brown.

Serve warm with applesauce, apple butter, fruit, or fruit puree.

〰Whole Wheat Waffles (for people who tolerate milk)〰

1 1/2 cups (360 milliliters) sifted whole wheat flour

2 teaspoons (10 milliliters) baking powder

1 egg, separated

1 1/2 cups (360 milliliters) milk

1/4 cup (60 milliliters) oil

1. In a measuring cup, combine flour and baking powder.

2. In a blender or large bowl, blend or beat together milk, egg yolk, and oil.

3. Add the dry ingredients, and beat again.

4. In a separate bowl, beat the egg white until light and fluffy. With a spoon, gently fold into the main mix. Do not use the machine for this step.

5. Preheat the waffle iron. Spray lightly with a cooking spray.

6. Scoop on dough. Cook the waffles about three minutes. Then turn them over, and cook the other side. You can tell they're ready to turn over when the top of the waffle iron does not stick and lets go easily.

Instead of syrup, try serving these warm and topped with applesauce, apple butter, fruit, or fruit puree. To make whole wheat pancakes, just reduce the amount of oil to 2 tablespoons (30 milliliters).

〰Shortbread Cookies〰

This will make about two dozen. Cut them into shapes for holidays. If your child suffers from wheat allergies, substitute barley flour for the whole wheat flour.

1 1/4 cup (300 milliliters) whole wheat flour

1/4 cup (60 milliliters) rice flour

1/4 teaspoon (2 milliliters) salt

1/2 cup (120 milliliters) butter

1/4 cup (60 milliliters) sugar

1. In a large measuring cup, sift together whole wheat flour, rice flour, and salt.

2. In a large bowl, cream together butter and sugar. Use an electric mixer if you wish.

3. Mix in the flour mixture. The dough will be dry and crumbly.

4. Knead lightly for a minute or two until the dough holds together. Form into a ball. Wrap in waxed paper or plastic wrap. Chill in refrigerator for a half hour—or longer, if you wish.

5. On a floured work surface, roll out thinly, to about 1/4 to 1/2 inch (about 1 centimeter) thick. Use cookie cutters to cut into shapes.

6. Transfer to a greased baking sheet. Bake at 325 degrees Fahrenheit (160 degrees Celsius) for about 20 minutes.

〰️Applesauce Oatmeal Cookies〰️

Oats and applesauce are both excellent foods for a growing child. And these soft cookies are delicious, besides. This recipe makes about three dozen. Since these cookies contain no milk, eggs, or flour, they can be especially welcome for children with allergic reactions.

3/4 cup (180 milliliters) oil

1 cup (240 milliliters) brown sugar

1 teaspoon (5 milliliters) vanilla extract

1/2 teaspoon (2 milliliters) salt

4 cups (just less than 1 liter) rolled oats

1 cup (240 milliliters) applesauce

1. In a large bowl, mix together oil, brown sugar, and vanilla extract. Use an electric mixer if you wish.

2. Mix in salt, oats, and applesauce.

3. Scoop by heaping spoonfuls onto a greased baking sheet. Flatten each cookie with the back of a spoon.

4. Bake at 325 degrees Fahrenheit (160 degrees Celsius) for about 30 minutes.

5. Cool on a wire rack, and store in tightly covered containers.

〰️Banana Oatmeal Cookies〰️

This is another soft, moist cookie, suitable for a toddler—and full of wholesome ingredients, including bananas, as a natural sweetener. This recipe makes about three dozen.

1 1/2 cups (360 milliliters) whole wheat flour

1 teaspoon (5 milliliters) baking powder

1/4 teaspoon (2 milliliters) baking soda

1/4 teaspoon (2 milliliters) cinnamon

1/4 teaspoon (2 milliliters) nutmeg

1 1/2 cups (360 milliliters) rolled oats

1/2 cup (120 milliliters or 1 stick) butter

1 cup (240 milliliters) brown sugar

2 eggs

1 cup (240 milliliters) banana slices (2 or 3 ripe bananas)

1. In a large measuring cup, sift together flour, baking powder, baking soda, cinnamon, and nutmeg. Stir in oats.

2. In a large bowl, cream together butter and brown sugar. Use an electric mixer if you wish. Mix in eggs, one at a time, and banana slices.

3. Mix in the flour-oatmeal mixture.

4. Scoop by heaping spoonfuls onto a greased baking sheet.

5. Bake at 350 degrees Fahrenheit (180 degrees Celsius) for about 12 minutes.

6. Cool on a wire rack, and store in a tightly covered container.

〰Rice Cookies〰

These could be ideal for a child with wheat allergies. The recipe creates about two dozen drop cookies.

1 cup (240 milliliters) rice flour

1/2 teaspoon (2 milliliters) baking powder

1/4 teaspoon (2 milliliters) baking soda

1/4 teaspoon (2 milliliters) salt

1/3 cup (80 milliliters) oil

1/2 cup (120 milliliters) honey or 1 cup (240 milliliters) sugar

1/2 teaspoon (2 milliliters) vanilla extract

1. In a large measuring cup, sift together rice flour, baking powder, baking soda, and salt.

2. In a large bowl, cream together oil, honey or sugar, and vanilla extract. Use an electric mixer if you wish.

3. Stir in the flour mixture.

4. Scoop by heaping spoonfuls onto a greased baking sheet.

5. Bake at 375 degrees Fahrenheit (190 degrees Celsius) for about 14 minutes.

6. Cool on a wire rack, and store in a tightly covered container.

〰Ginger Snaps〰

Maybe these are called "snaps," because they're thin, crispy cookies and can snap in your hands. This makes about three dozen. Cut them into shapes for holidays.

3 cups (720 milliliters) sifted enriched, unbleached all-purpose flour

1 teaspoon (5 milliliters) baking soda

1 teaspoon (5 milliliters) ground ginger

1/2 teaspoon (2 milliliters) salt

1/3 cup (80 milliliters) brown sugar

1 cup (240 milliliters or 2 sticks) butter

2/3 cup (160 milliliters) molasses

1. In a large bowl, combine flour, baking soda, ginger, salt, and brown sugar.

2. Use a pastry blender or two forks to cut in the butter, until the mix has a breadcrumb-like consistency.

3. Stir in molasses.

4. Knead for a minute or two until the dough holds together. Form into a ball. Wrap in waxed paper or plastic wrap. Chill for half an hour—or longer, if you wish.

5. On a floured work surface, roll out thinly, to about 1/4 to 1/2 inch (about 1 centimeter) thick. Use cookie cutters to cut into shapes.

6. Transfer to a greased baking sheet. Bake at 350 degrees Fahrenheit (180 degrees Celsius) for 10 to 12 minutes.

7. Cool on a wire rack, and store in a tightly covered container.

🥖Johnny Cake🥖

The name "Johnny Cake" may have started out as "journey cake," good food that keeps well over a long journey. It's cornmeal, without too much sweetening, and you serve it without frosting.

1 cup (240 milliliters) unbleached, enriched white flour

3/4 cup (180 milliliters) non-degerminated cornmeal

1/2 teaspoon (2 milliliters) baking soda

1 teaspoon (5 milliliters) cream of tartar

1/8 teaspoon (2 milliliters) salt

1 tablespoon (15 milliliters) butter

1/4 cup (60 milliliters) honey or 1/3 cup (80 milliliters) sugar

1 tablespoon (15 milliliters) molasses

1 egg

1 cup (240 milliliters) milk

1. In a large measuring cup, sift flour, and combine with cornmeal, baking soda, cream of tartar, and salt.

2. Melt the butter. This is a good use for a microwave.

3. In a large bowl, cream together the butter, honey or sugar, and molasses. Use an electric mixer if you wish.

4. Beat the egg. Then mix the egg and milk into the large bowl.

5. Stir in the dry ingredients.

6. Pour the batter into a greased 8-inch (20-centimeter) square pan.

7. Bake at 425 degrees Fahrenheit (220 degrees Celsius) for about 25 minutes. It's done when a toothpick comes out clean.

8. Cool in the pan for a few minutes. Then transfer to a wire rack. You may want to serve this warm.

🥖Applesauce Cake🥖

This makes a one-layer cake. It could be just right for a first birthday celebration.

1 cup (240 milliliters) whole wheat flour

1 teaspoon (5 milliliters) baking soda

1/2 teaspoon (2 milliliters) baking powder

1/2 teaspoon (2 milliliters) cinnamon

1/2 teaspoon (2 milliliters) cloves

1/2 cup (120 milliliters) oil

1 cup (240 milliliters) brown sugar

1 egg

1 cup (240 milliliters) applesauce

1/2 cup (120 milliliters) raisins, if you wish

1. In a large measuring cup, sift together flour, baking soda, baking powder, cinnamon, and cloves.

2. In a large bowl, cream together oil and sugar. Use an electric mixer if you wish. Mix in the egg and applesauce.

3. Mix in the flour mixture.

4. If you wish, stir in raisins by hand.

5. Pour the batter into a greased 8-inch (20-centimeter) round cake pan. Bake at 350 degrees Fahrenheit (180 degrees Celsius) for 50 minutes.

6. Cool in the pan for a few minutes. Then transfer to a wire rack, and cool completely.

7. Frost, or sprinkle with confectioner's sugar. Or serve with—what else—applesauce. See recipes for frosting, pages 152 and 173.

☞First Birthday Cupcakes (for people who tolerate milk☜)

Make a dozen cupcakes for a special first birthday.

1 cup (240 milliliters) unbleached, enriched all-purpose flour

1 teaspoon (5 milliliters) baking soda

1/2 teaspoon (2 milliliters) cinnamon

1/2 teaspoon (2 milliliters) ground ginger

1/8 teaspoon (1 milliliter) salt

1/2 cup (120 milliliters or one stick) butter

3/4 cup (180 milliliters) honey or 1 cup (240 milliliters) sugar

2 eggs

2/3 cup (160 milliliters) sour cream

1. In a large measuring cup, sift together flour, baking soda, cinnamon, ground ginger, and salt.

2. In a large bowl, cream together butter and honey or sugar. Use an electric mixer if you wish.

3. Beat in the eggs.

4. Mix in dry ingredients, alternately with the sour cream.

5. Spoon into 12 muffin cups, so that each is about two-thirds full. Bake at 350 degrees Fahrenheit (180 degrees Celsius) for 25 minutes.

6. Transfer to a wire rack, and cool completely.

First Birthday Frosting

If you wish to avoid too much sweetening, you can always frost a cake with apple butter or fruit puree. But here's a light frosting that looks and tastes more like traditional cake frosting, enough fo a dozen cupcakes or a one-layer cake.

1/2 cup (120 milliliters) nonfat dry milk powder

1/2 cup (120 milliliters) ice water

1 teaspoon (5 milliliters) honey or 2 teaspoons sugar

1/2 teaspoon (2 milliliters) vanilla extract

1. Whip the milk powder with ice water. Use an electric mixer if you wish.

2. Whip in honey or sugar and vanilla extract, until light and fluffy.

Chapter Twenty-Two
Fats, Oils & Spreads

You know that people shouldn't eat too much fat. The message is all around us. But people are, mostly, ignoring the message.

In any case, the problem is more complicated than just avoiding fat, and the issue of fat in the diet has aroused more controversy than just about any other. It's difficult to know what to do when food is full of fat—and food packages are covered with labels that sound as if they're straight from a science laboratory, with dubious connection to real life.

First, fats, oils, and sweets are at the very top of the Food Pyramid. That visual image of a very small, disappearing amount of space is meant to indicate that there ought to be little room in the diet for these substances. They should be used "sparingly," the US Department of Agriculture suggests. But that makes it seem as if all fats and oils are the same, lumped together at the point of the food pyramid.

In fact, some fats are highly necessary for the growth of small babies. Mother's milk is full of fat, the right sort of fat, perfect for babies. When a baby is ready for cow's milk, almost all the experts recommend whole milk rather than the low-fat or nonfat milk popular with older people.

Certainly, a low-fat diet is of value in avoiding obesity, heart disease, and other ailments plaguing modern humanity. As the most concentrated source of calories, fat in the diet creates obesity as surely as sugar causes obesity. An ounce or gram of fat contains over twice as many calories as an ounce or gram of protein or carbohydrate. Also, calories from fat are absorbed and stored as fat more quickly than other calories.

And all too many people have developed a "fat tooth." They relish high-fat foods such as French fries, potato chips, heavily marbled steaks, pastries, and candy bars.

Your baby does not relish fat, refined sugar, or salt, and fortunately has no way of knowing that these are the modern eating addictions. You have the opportunity to avoid allowing your baby to become accustomed to fatty or greasy foods.

But it is not a simple matter of avoiding all fats, especially when feeding a baby or toddler. It's more a matter of avoiding the bad fats and embracing the right, good fats.

Fat content is another reason to make and bake your own. Then you know what sort of fat is in your food—and how much.

Go for good fats.

Here's an easy rule to remember when you buy fats or foods with fat content.

- If it moves, it may not be so bad.
- If it doesn't move, it's bad.

This is an oversimplification. But in general, the fat that is worst for you tends to be solid at room temperature. It is like sludge, and it can act like sludge in your circulatory system. Think of lard or the fat marbled within a steak.

The fats that are best for you tend to be liquid at room temperature. Essentially, they can flow through your circulatory system, without piling up or sticking. Think of olive oil.

Go for good oils.

Here are some of the best oils to use in cooking or on salads:

- Canola
- Flaxseed
- Olive (cold-pressed, virgin, or extra virgin)*
- Pumpkin seed
- Soy bean

Here are medium-level—and commonly used—oils:

- Corn
- Safflower
- Sesame
- Sunflower
- Peanut

Here are some of the worst:

- Coconut
- Cottonseed
- Palm kernel

* *Do not use olive oil for baking. Its strong, somewhat fruity taste overpowers other flavors.*

Buying guide for fats and oils.

- Read the labels on fat content in packaged foods. As a general rule, avoid "hydrogenated fat," "partially hydrogenated fat," or anything like "trans fats" or "trans fatty acids." Look for labels that say "no trans fatty acids" or "free of saturated fats." There's a lot of verbal cover-up in labels about fat content. For example, "vegetable oil" sounds good, but that labeling doesn't tell you anything real. Another meaningless term is "cholesterol free." It doesn't necessarily translate to good.

- Do not buy anything containing olestra. Olestra is an indigestible factory-made fat, with just too much bad news surrounding it. Consider that it's still in the experimental stage, and the experiment is not going well.

- As you can afford it, you may wish to buy unsalted butter rather than margarines or shortening. Margarine is at least 80 percent vegetable oils, usually with milk added, rather than the 80 percent to nearly 100 percent creamy fat of butter. But margarines, once thought to be more healthful than butter, tend these days to contain more and more unknown quantities. Butter is at least somewhat natural, compared to the increasingly unnatural margarines and imitation margarines. You need a nutrition scientist at your elbow when you choose margarines these days. When you buy margarine, you're buying a mystery.

- Consider trying whipped butter. That's butter with air or inert gas incorporated to make it light and soft. Whipped butter sells in tubs for use as a spread. However, don't use soft, whipped butter or margarine in recipes for baked goods, since it's difficult to gauge the correct measurement. And don't use them for sautéing or pan-frying, since they burn too quickly. (You may want to experiment some time with making your own butter or whipped butter. See pages 156-157.)

- If possible, buy peanut butter or other nut butters without added sugar and fats other than the natural fat of the nuts. (Or make your own peanut butter, page 157.)

- As possible, avoid preservatives, BHA (butylated hydroxyansiole) and BHT (butylated hydroxytoluene).

Make good food less fatty and greasy.

- Make your own dips, spreads, and salad dressings so you can control the amount and type of fat.

- Find substitutes for high-fat foods. For example, use a topping of apple butter, fruit puree, or cottage cheese instead of syrup, butter, or margarine. Your own baked goods are almost guaranteed to contain higher quality fat and less fat than commercial cookies, cakes, and snacks.

- Cut down on the need for cooking oil or grease by using a lubricant to spray pots and pans. Lecithin is a pure vegetable derivative that you can buy in a spray form.

• Choose cooking methods that avoid grease. Try cooking with a minimum of grease and a maximum of good nutrition. For example, instead of pan-frying meats, broil them in the oven. You can put them on a rack that allows fat to drip off into a pan beneath. You can brown meats the same way. Or try slow-cooking, poaching, steaming, or baking.

~Your Own Butter (for people who tolerate milk)~

You don't need an old-fashioned churn if you want to see what it's like to make butter. You can "churn" butter by hand or—easier by far—with an electric mixer. This is a lot like whipping cream. You may have noticed that when you whip cream, sometimes the process does not go well. The cream forms bubbles, and you can no longer get a good volume of foam. Those bubbles are the beginning of butter.

1. Pour heavy fresh cream or whipping cream into the large bowl of an electric mixer. Let it sit until it reaches room temperatures, or cooler. The ideal temperature for churning is 55 to 65 degrees Fahrenheit (12 to 18 degrees Celsius). (Temperature is one reason, besides the messiness involved with a traditional churn, that small boys were once sent outside to churn butter.)

2. Beat until the cream is no longer forming foam but is separating into small clumps. When it finally forms a semisolid mass, separate from a small amount of liquid, you're finished.

3. Pour off the buttermilk, and rinse the butter. Press the butter with a wooden spoon or your hands to remove more of the water and make it more solid.

4. Form the butter into a lump, and wrap it well. You can keep it in the refrigerator for a week or more, or it freezes well.

You're probably used to the ease of measuring sticks of commercial butter or margarine. To measure a lump of butter, use the water displacement method. If you want 1/2 cup butter (equivalent to one stick, or 120 milliliters), fill a large measuring cup with 1/2 cup (120 milliliters) cold water. Add butter until the water reaches the one-cup mark. Then just drain off the water. You're left with the right amount of butter.

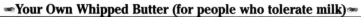

➾Your Own Whipped Butter (for people who tolerate milk)➾

You can lower the fat content of butter while retaining its good taste by whipping butter. Use this only as a spread, not as an ingredient in baking. It's too difficult to get a correct measure for baking. Use an electric mixer, blender, or food processor. You can multiply this recipe to whip up any amount.

1/2 cup (1 stick or 120 milliliters) butter

1/2 cup water

1. Cut the butter into pieces, and let it soften at room temperature, or no more than 20 seconds in the microwave oven. Ideal temperature is 55 to 65 degrees Fahrenheit (12 to 18 degrees Celsius).

2. Heat the water to just below boiling, 30 seconds or so in the microwave oven.

3. Put the butter and water into an electric mixer, blender, or food processor. Blend until creamy and fluffy. (It will also turn a paler color.)

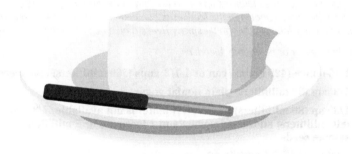

➾Your Own Peanut Butter (for people who tolerate nuts)➾

You can make actual peanut butter. This is the real stuff without all the additions and chemicals of commercial peanut butter. You'll need a food processor or heavy-duty blender.

1 cup (240 milliliters) peanuts

1 tablespoon (15 milliliters) peanut or other vegetable oil

1. Put peanuts and oil in the food processor or blender, and process.

2. Stop every 30 seconds to scrape the sides of the machine.

3. You get to decide how chunky or smooth you want your peanut butter, and whether you want to add salt.

As a variation, try making pecan or walnut butters. Or mix in some pureed cooked carrots for an unusual peanut-carrot butter.

〰️Cottage Cheese Spread (for people who tolerate milk)〰️

This is a spread for sandwiches or crackers, more nutritious than butter or margarine. Your child wil
probably like the cottage cheese taste. Use a blender or food processor.

1 cup (240 milliliters) cottage cheese

⅓ cup (80 milliliters) milk

Fruit, if you wish

1. Place cottage cheese and milk in a blender or food processor, and
blend thoroughly. You may wish to add another tablespoon or two of
milk, until the mixture forms a spreadable consistency.

2. Chill in a sealed container. If you wish, stir in fruit by hand, just as
you serve this.

〰️Hummus for Young People (for people who tolerate milk)〰️

Recently, hummus has become a popular spread and dip for people who are careful with their diets
It's a puree of chickpeas, flavored with sesame seed (usually in the form of the seed paste, tahini),
and lemon. Since hummus originated in the Mediterranean countries, it's often spiced with garlic,
cumin, paprika, and occasionally other hotter spices. Here's a mild version suitable for children.

Use a food processor or heavy-duty blender.

1 15-ounce (420 grams) can or 1 1/2 cups (360 milliliters) chickpeas

1/3 cup (80 milliliters) plain nonfat yogurt

**1/3 cup (80 milliliters) tahini or, if tahini is not available, 1/3 cup
(80 milliliters) additional yogurt and 1 teaspoon or 5 milliliters
sesame seeds**

1 tablespoon (15 milliliters) lemon juice

1 tablespoon (15 milliliters) olive oil

1. Drain canned chickpeas. Or put dry chickpeas in water, and bring
to boil. Then simmer until tender.

2. In food processor or blender, place yogurt, tahini or additional
yogurt and sesame seeds, lemon juice, and olive oil. Process until
smooth.

3. Add chickpeas. Process 30 seconds. Then stop and scrape the
sides of the machine. Process another 30 seconds. Keep going until
smooth.

4. Serve with pita bread, dry toast, crackers, or veggies. For adults,
stir in 1/4 teaspoon (2 milliliters) minced garlic, and sprinkle with
paprika.

〰Your Own Apple Butter〰

This apple butter contains no butter or other fats. Children often prefer apple butter to spreads much less nutritious. If you don't want to spend a lot of time peeling apples, then use a food mill. Boil two one-pint (half liter) or four half-pint (quarter liter) jars in water to sterilize. Have them ready as containers to hold about a quart of your own apple butter.

4 quarts (4 liters) apples

1 quart (1 liter) fresh cider or unsweetened apple juice

2 tablespoons (30 milliliters) lemon juice, if you wish

1 tablespoon (15 milliliters) cinnamon, if you wish

1. In a large saucepan, boil the cider or apple juice. Boil gently until the liquid is reduced to about half its former volume.

2. Cut each apple in quarters, and remove the cores. You don't need to peel.

3. Add the apples to the reduced cider. Cover, and lower the heat. Simmer and stir occasionally until the apples are soft and tender.

4. Put a food mill over a large bowl. Carefully spoon the apples into the food mill. Turn the crank, so that the mill pushes the apples down into the bowl. That removes the peels.

5. Return the apple mash to the pan. Simmer, uncovered, until the apple mash thickens. Stir occasionally. The apple butter is finished when it is so thick that when you raise some in a spoon, it plops back in, almost forming a sheet as it plops.

6. If you wish, stir in lemon juice and cinnamon.

7. Spoon into sterilized jars, and seal.

Chapter Twenty-Three
Fun Food for Toddlers

You can prepare food for toddlers that's child-attractive and still nutritious. These recipes allow a few "grown-up" ingredients such as a taste of spices, some onion, tomatoes, and moderate sweetening.

As always, when you make your own food, you hold the advantage. You can control the ingredients. You know what's in the foods you serve. You can watch out for allergies, indigestion, or other unpleasant reactions. You keep track of what's happening.

All of these recipes are suitable for the whole family. We certainly hope that older children and adults will like them, and a few may be suitable for children a bit under one year old, at least those who don't have allergic reactions and who can chew and swallow well.

But for the most part, these are foods created for and attractive to those busy, sometimes cantankerous and opinionated little people, our one-, two-, and three-year-olds.

Tips for the toddler's chief chef and food manager.

- This is the time when independent-minded toddlers begin to take charge of food as well as everything else in their environment. Do your best to guide these natural instincts in positive, happy directions.

- Try, as best you can, to establish definite times for meals and snacks. Otherwise, food can all too easily become a continuous parade of handouts and demands, with more handouts and more demands. It's not easy, but attempt to allow a child to become hungry and then eat, rather than just eat and drink without real hunger.

- Try, as best you can, to avoid rushed meals. Let a toddler take time to enjoy food and satisfy hunger. Don't ordinarily allow eating in the car or on the run. Even little people should learn to sit down and eat without hurry. It's safer, as well as more polite.

- As you can, begin letting your toddlers help with kitchen projects. You can help them satisfy their inherent curiosity and develop their own natural creativity. Perhaps they can help make grocery store selections or help in the garden.

- Offer small servings. Large quantities can overwhelm a child. You can always serve a second helping.

- If your child does not like vegetables, assume it's temporary. You may be able to grate or dice a few vegetables into mild dishes such as cottage cheese, macaroni and cheese, or rice.

Ideas for colorful tidbits and nutritious nibbles.

Some toddlers enjoy small bites of several foods arranged in separate little compartments, such as a divided tray or dish, an ice cube tray, or a muffin tin. Usually, the more colorful the bite, the more attractive it is to eat. Probably the very small portions also add to the attraction. You can prepare a nibble set quickly with bits and scraps of leftover fruits, vegetables, and baked goods. You may want to serve the tray with a small dipping dish.

Here are some suggestions for colorful bites for a toddler's food tray:

- Several blueberries, perhaps frozen
- A cantaloupe or watermelon ball
- A cherry
- A couple of grapes or raisins
- A strawberry
- A pineapple chunk
- An orange or tangerine section
- An apple quarter
- A plum half
- A celery slice
- A carrot curl or two, or a couple of carrot sticks
- A cucumber or zucchini slice
- A broccoli floret
- A strip of green pepper
- A piece of rice cake
- Pieces of dry cereal, chow mein noodles, or potato sticks
- A couple of cheese cubes
- A wedge of hard-boiled egg

Ideas for dip dishes.

Some of these dips are good as spreads on crackers or toast. Each of these makes between 1/4 cup (60 milliliters) to 1 cup (240 milliliters). Some are best made with a blender or food processor. Some stir up with a spoon.

1. 1/2 cup (120 milliliters) cottage cheese, with 1/4 cup (60 milliliters) applesauce or fruit preserves blended or stirred in.

2. 1/2 cup (120 milliliters) cottage cheese, blended with 2 tablespoons (30 milliliters) milk or juice.

3. 1/4 cup (60 milliliters) yogurt, blended with 1/4 cup (60 milliliters) natural cheese pieces and 1/4 cup (60 milliliters) cream cheese.

4. 1/4 cup (60 milliliters) yogurt, blended with 1/4 (60 milliliters) cup soft tofu and 1/4 cup (60 milliliters) natural cheese pieces.

5. 1/4 cup (60 milliliters) yogurt, blended with 1/4 cup (60 milliliters) orange juice.

6. 1/4 cup (60 milliliters) cream cheese, softened, with 2 tablespoons (30 milliliters) milk or juice stirred in.

7. 3 tablespoons (45 milliliters) ketchup with 1 tablespoon (15 milliliters) flax oil stirred in.

8. 1 avocado, peeled, stoned, and cut into pieces, blended smooth, with 2 tablespoons (30 milliliters) lemon juice

Ideas for fun food.

1. Cut vegetables into shapes such as cucumber wheels, carrot curls, or green pepper zigzags.

2. Peel and cut in half a pear or a peach. Spread with yogurt, and decorate with dry cereal, banana slices, blueberries, raisins, carrot curls, or parsley.

3. Spread a cracker with peanut butter and decorate with dry cereal, banana slices, blueberries, raisins, or carrot curls.

4. Decorate applesauce with dry cereal, banana slices, blueberries, or raisins.

5. Tint a small amount of milk with food coloring. Use it to paint toast or cookies.

6. Use a cookie cutter to cut toasted cheese or other thin sandwiches into shapes.

7. Write a message, and wrap it tightly in aluminum foil. Punch a small hole in the top of the foil, and tie on a ribbon with a fancy bow. Push the message into the top of a cupcake. The bow stays on top for pulling out later.

⬲Banana Boats (for people who tolerate nuts)⬲

Toddler may like fruit best when it's frozen and presented as a fancy banana boat, especially if they get to help decorate it.

Banana

Peanut butter

Pineapple, orange, or other fruit, peeled and cut into chunks or sections

Frozen yogurt, if you wish

Bran cereal or nut pieces, if you wish

1. Peel the banana, and split it lengthwise. Spread it with peanut butter, and put it together as a sandwich.

2. Wrap in plastic or foil, and freeze.

3. Arrange the frozen banana boats on dessert dishes. Arrange pineapple chunks, orange sections, or other fruit on top.

4. If you wish, top with frozen yogurt, and sprinkle on bran cereal or nut pieces.

⬲Colorful Fruit Salad⬲

This is a version of Waldorf salad for young people. If you think your toddler might like an unusual salad, make it with cottage cheese rather than yogurt, and serve it in a whole-wheat pita.

Apple

Grapes

Celery

Yogurt or cottage cheese

1. Peel, core, and cut up an apple. Cut grapes and celery into small pieces.

2. Stir apple, grapes, and celery into a dish of yogurt or cottage cheese.

⬲Colorful Veggie Salad⬲

Toddlers often don't like the texture of lettuce. Here's a colorful salad that they may favor instead. Include onions and tomatoes only if your child already tolerates them well.

Green pepper

Red pepper

Yellow pepper

Onion

Tomato

Lemon juice

1. Wash and cut the peppers into strips. Chop the onion and tomato.

2. Toss with a bit of lemon juice. Or adults may prefer a vinaigrette dressing.

Peanut Butter Soup (for people who tolerate nuts)

2 tablespoons (30 milliliters) butter

1 tablespoon (15 milliliters) flour

1/4 cup (60 milliliters) peanut butter

2 cups (480 milliliters) whole milk

1. Melt the butter in a large saucepan.

2. Remove the pan from the heat, and blend in flour and peanut butter.

3. Return to medium heat, and slowly stir in the milk.

4. Continue heating, and stir constantly, until the soup boils.

Toddler's First Pizza (for people who tolerate milk)

Your child is going to know about pizza all too soon. But don't serve the greasy, sleazy kind. Serve an English muffin as a mini-pizza just perfect for one serving. Your toddler may even be able to do some creative pizza decorating.

English muffin

2 tablespoons (30 milliliters) tomato sauce per muffin

A light sprinkling of oregano and basil, if you wish

Shredded cheese

1. Top the English muffin with tomato sauce, a sprinkling of oregano and basil, and a topping of shredded cheese. If you wish to use up some leftovers, you could add a small amount of ground beef, chopped onion, or green pepper strips.

2. Toast in a toaster oven. Or bake at 350 degrees Fahrenheit (180 degrees Celsius) for five minutes. Or heat on high power in a microwave oven for two minutes. The mini-pizza should be hot and bubbly.

Or use a rice cake as the basis for a first pizza-like experience.

≈One Pizza Per Person (for people who tolerate milk)≈

Make four small pizzas, each one great for one serving. This is a yeast dough, so leave enough time for it to rise.

1 tablespoon (one packet or 15 milliliters) active dry yeast

1 teaspoon (5 milliliters) sugar or diastatic malt powder

3 tablespoons (45 milliliters) warm water

2 tablespoons (30 milliliters) butter

5 tablespoons (75 milliliters) milk

2 cups (480 milliliters) whole wheat flour (or mix whole wheat and white), sifted

1. In a small bowl, dissolve yeast and sugar or malt powder in warm water. Let this bowl stand in a warm place for a few minutes, while you prepare the rest. If the yeast is good and active, it should turn bubbly and puff up a bit.

2. Melt the butter. This is a good use for a microwave.

3. In a large bowl, stir together butter, milk, and the yeast mixture.

4. Then add the flour, and stir until the dough begins to come together.

5. Turn the dough onto a lightly floured surface. Knead for a few minutes until it forms a smooth ball and becomes less sticky.

6. Place in a large greased bowl. (You can use the same bowl you used to mix.) Cover with a clean kitchen towel, and put into a warm place. Let rise for one hour.

7. Punch down. Turn onto a lightly floured surface. Divide into four pieces, and shape each into a ball. Flatten so that each ball forms a circle about 8 inches (20 centimeters) in diameter. Transfer the balls to a greased baking sheet.

8. Top with your choice of pizza toppings. For example, spread with tomato sauce. Then sprinkle on oregano. Arrange a choice such as cut-up green peppers, chopped onion, cooked ground beef. Top with shredded cheese.

9. Bake at 400 degrees Fahrenheit (200 degrees Celsius) for 20 to 25 minutes.

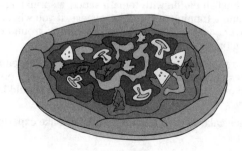

❧Colorful Cubes❧

Gelatin cubes are the all-time favorite toddler finger food. Choose a colorful fruit juice, such as orange, grape, or cranberry.

2 tablespoons (30 milliliters or two packets) unflavored gelatin

2 cups (480 milliliters) fruit juice

1. In a small heatproof bowl, sprinkle the gelatin over one cup (240 milliliters) fruit juice. Stir.

2. Heat on high power in the microwave oven for one minute, or until just short of boiling. Stir to dissolve the gelatin.

3. Stir in the rest of the fruit juice.

4. Pour into an 8-inch (20-centimeter) square glass baking dish.

5. Refrigerate until completely set.

6. Cut into cubes. Or cut into shapes with a cookie cutter. Set in a pan of warm water for a few seconds until the cubes slide out easily.

❧Veggie or Fruit Gelatin❧

Your toddler may find gelatin with vegetables and fruits more attractive than vegetables or fruits alone.

1/4 cup (60 milliliters) water

1 tablespoon (15 milliliters) unflavored gelatin

1 1/4 cups (300 milliliters) fruit juice or water

1/2 cup (120 milliliters) grated carrots or 1/2 cup (120 milliliters) grated apples or 1/2 cup (120 milliliters) cottage cheese

2 tablespoons (30 milliliters) raisins, if you wish

1. Heat the water in a microwave oven to near boiling. Stir in gelatin to dissolve.

2. Pour fruit juice or water into a large pan or mold. Stir in the gelatin mixture.

3. Refrigerate until partially set.

4. Gently fold in your choice of grated carrots, grated apples, or cottage cheese. If you wish, stir in raisins.

5. Refrigerate until set.

☞Potato Pancakes☜

These potato pancakes are traditional for Hanukkah, but they're good any time, and toddlers seem to like the texture.

4 large potatoes

2 eggs

2 tablespoons (30 milliliters) flour, cracker crumbs, or matzo meal

2 tablespoons (30 milliliters) oil

1 medium onion

1/4 teaspoon (2 milliliters) pepper, if you wish

1/4 teaspoon (2 milliliters) salt, if you wish

2 tablespoons (30 milliliters) chopped chives, if you wish

1. Peel the potatoes. Use a grater to grate them. Or else cut them into chunks, and put in a food processor. Pulse the machine only once or twice to grate. Place the grated potatoes in a colander or strainer to drain off the liquid.

2. Separate the eggs. Put the yolks into a large bowl, and beat slightly. Stir in flour, crumbs, or matzo, and oil.

3. Chop the onion to 1/4 to 1/2 cup (60-120 milliliters). Add to the mixture, along with the grated potatoes. If you wish, add pepper, salt, and chives.

4. In the small bowl of an electric mixer, beat the egg whites until they form stiff peaks.

5. Gently fold into the potato mixture.

6. Preheat a griddle until it is hot enough that a drop of water bounces a bit on it. Spoon on the pancake batter. Leave space between the pancakes so they can expand. When you see bubbles form and begin to pop, flip the pancakes, and cook the other side, until brown.

Serve warm with applesauce, apple butter, fruit, or fruit puree.

☞Granola Mix☜

You can serve this for breakfast with milk and fruit. Or serve it by itself as a favorite snack. Or you can make it into bars or cookies. If your child does not tolerate nuts, simply leave out the nuts. You can create any number of variations. For any ingredient you don't want, substitute dry cereal, shredded coconut, or dried apple pieces.

4 cups (1 liter) rolled oats

1 cup (240 milliliters) wheat germ

1 cup (240 milliliters) sunflower or sesame seeds (or a combination)

1 cup (240 milliliters) unsalted peanuts or almonds

1 teaspoon (5 milliliters) cinnamon

1/2 teaspoon (2 milliliters) nutmeg

1 teaspoon (5 milliliters) vanilla extract

1/2 cup (120 milliliters) honey

1/2 cup (120 milliliters) oil

1 cup (240 milliliters) raisins

1. In a large bowl, mix by hand the rolled oats, wheat germ, sunflower or sesame seeds, peanuts or almonds, cinnamon, nutmeg, and vanilla extract.

2. Combine the honey and oil, and heat. This is a good use for a microwave oven.

3. Stir the honey and oil mix into the large bowl.

4. Spread onto a baking sheet or jelly roll pan.

5. Bake at 225 degrees Fahrenheit (110 degrees Celsius) for about 30 minutes.

6. Stir in the raisins.

7. Cool and store in a tightly covered container.

☙Granola Bars☙

You can cut this into about three dozen granola bars. Do not use an electric mixer for this recipe. This makes a stiff, dry dough, so a wooden spoon is best for stirring it well.

1 cup (240 milliliters) whole wheat flour

1 teaspoon (5 milliliters) baking soda

4 cups (1 liter) granola mix

3/4 cup (1 1/2 sticks or 180 milliliters) butter

2 eggs

1 teaspoon (5 milliliters) vanilla extract

1. In a large bowl, sift together flour and baking soda. Stir in the granola mix.

2. Melt the butter. This is a good use for a microwave oven.

3. Beat the eggs lightly. In a small bowl, combine butter, eggs, and vanilla extract.

4. Pour the butter mix over the dry ingredients. Mix by hand.

5. Press into a large rectangular baking dish or a jelly roll pan, about 10 x 15 inches (25 x 40 centimenters). Press the dough flat with the back of a spoon.

6. Bake at 375 degrees Fahrenheit (190 degrees Celsius) for about 20 minutes.

7. While warm, cut into about 36 granola bars. Then cool in the pan.

⇝Granola Cookies⇜

This makes about 30 cookies.

1 1/4 cups (300 milliliters) whole wheat flour

1 teaspoon (5 milliliters) baking powder

1 teaspoon (5 milliliters) cinnamon

1 cup (240 milliliters) granola mix

1/3 cup (80 milliliters) butter

1 cup (240 milliliters) brown sugar

1 egg

1 teaspoon (5 milliliters) vanilla extract

1. In a large measuring cup, sift together flour, baking powder, and cinnamon. Stir in granola mix.

2. In a large bowl, cream together butter and brown sugar. Use an electric mixer if you wish.

3. Beat the egg, and stir it and the vanilla extract into the butter-sugar mix.

4. Stir in the dry ingredients.

5. Spoon onto a greased baking sheet in heaping teaspoonfuls.

6. Bake at 350 degrees Fahrenheit for about 12 minutes.

7. Cool on a wire rack, and store in a tightly covered container.

⇝Yogurt Pops (for people who tolerate milk)⇜

Use popsicle molds, or else small paper cups with plastic spoons as sticks. Here's what you need for four molds or cups. Feel free to be creative.

1 cup (240 milliliters) yogurt

1/2 cup (120 milliliters) mashed bananas, mashed strawberries, fruit puree, or fruit juice

1. Freeze (or partially thaw) yogurt to a soft mush.

2. Beat in fruit or fruit juice.

3. Spoon into molds or cups. Partially freeze the pops, so you can insert the sticks or spoons to stand upright.

4. Return to freeze solid.

5. To serve the pops, set the molds in a pan of warm water for a few seconds until the pop slides out easily. Or else peel away the paper cup.

≈Sorbet≈

Sorbet is a frozen fruit dessert, just right for a hot summer's day, and more nutritious than ice cream. Use a blender or food processor. To make this quickly, use pre-packaged frozen fruit, such as strawberries, raspberries, or peaches.

1 tablespoon (15 milliliters) sugar

1 tablespoon (15 milliliters) water

2 cups (470 milliliters) fresh or frozen fruit

2 tablespoons (30 milliliters) lemon juice

1. In a small cup or bowl, stir sugar into water. Chill while you prepare the fruit.

2. If you are using fresh fruit, peel and cut it into chunks. Place in blender or food processor, and puree until smooth.

3. Pour in sugar-water and lemon juice. Puree once more until smooth.

4. Pour into a shallow bowl or pan, and freeze until slushy, about two hours.

5. Spoon the slush into the blender or food processor. Blend until smooth, less than ten seconds.

6. Freeze until firm. Scoop into dessert dishes.

≈Baked Apple Crunch≈

This is a traditional crunchy-apple dessert. Toddlers like it when they begin to like experimenting with different textures.

About 8 apples

1 cup (240 milliliters) rolled oats

1/2 cup (120 milliliters) brown sugar

1 teaspoon (5 milliliters) cinnamon

1/2 cup (120 milliliters) hot water

1 teaspoon (5 milliliters) lemon juice

1. Peel, core, and slice the apples to make about four cups (1 liter).

2. In a small bowl, stir together rolled oats, brown sugar, and cinnamon.

3. Arrange about half the apples in a 1 1/2–quart (1.5 liters) casserole dish or in an 8- x 8-inch (20- x 20-centimeter) baking dish.

4. Spread a layer of about half the oatmeal mixture.

5. Arrange the rest of the apples on top.

6. Spread a layer of the rest of the oatmeal mixture.

7. Pour on hot water, and sprinkle on lemon juice.

8. Bake at 375 degrees Fahrenheit (190 degrees Celsius) for 40 to 45 minutes.

❦Gingerbread People❦

When they're old enough, your children will love decorating these gingerbread people. Or of course, you can make them in any shape you wish. Depending on how thick you roll the dough and how large you cut your shapes, this recipe makes about 15 people.

2 1/4 cups (540 milliliters) whole wheat or enriched white flour

1 teaspoon (5 milliliters) baking powder

¼ teaspoon (2 milliliters) baking soda

1 teaspoon (5 milliliters) ginger

1/4 teaspoon (2 milliliters) cinnamon

1/4 cup (60 milliliters) butter

1/3 cup (80 milliliters) brown sugar

1/3 cup (80 milliliters) molasses

1/3 cup (80 milliliters) milk

1. In a large measuring cup, sift together flour, baking powder, baking soda, ginger, and cinnamon.

2. Melt the butter. This is a good use for a microwave oven.

3. In a large bowl, mix together melted butter, brown sugar, and milk. Use an electric mixer if you wish.

4. Stir in the dry ingredients, alternately with the milk. You'll have to finish working in the flour with your hands. This is supposed to be a dry, stiff dough.

5. Roll out on a lightly floured surface, and cut out shapes.

6. Before baking, decorate with raisin bits and preserved or candied fruits. Transfer to a baking sheet.

7. Bake at 350 degrees Fahrenheit (180 degrees Celsius) for about eight minutes. The cookies are done when a toothpick comes out clean.

8. Cool on a wire rack. When the shapes are cool, finish decorating. Make icing for decorating by combining 1/4 cup (60 milliliters) confectioner's sugar with a few drops water and, if you wish, food coloring. Decorate by using a toothpick, small plastic spoon, or small knife.

☞Second-Birthday Carrot Cake☜

Of course, you can make this cake to celebrate any birthday or holiday. And it's infinitely more delicious and nutritious than the commercial variety. This makes a one-layer cake.

4 or 5 medium carrots

1 1/2 cups (360 milliliters) unbleached, enriched white flour

1 teaspoon (5 milliliters) cinnamon

1 teaspoon (5 milliliters) baking powder

1 teaspoon (5 milliliters) baking soda

1/2 teaspoon (2 milliliters) salt

1/2 cup (120 milliliters) oil

1/2 cup (120 milliliters) honey or 1 cup (240 milliliters) sugar

2 eggs

1 teaspoon (5 milliliters) vanilla extract

1. Peel the carrots. Grate them with a grater or a food processor to make two cups (480 milliliters).

2. In a large measuring cup, sift together flour, cinnamon, baking powder, baking soda, and salt.

3. In a food processor, heavy-duty blender, or electric mixer, cream together the oil and honey or sugar.

4. Blend in eggs and vanilla extract.

5. Blend in dry ingredients, alternately with the grated carrots.

6. Transfer to a square baking dish, 9- x 9-inches (22- x 22-centimeters).

7. Bake at 375 degrees Fahrenheit (190 degrees Celsius) for 30 to 35 minutes.

8. Cool in the pan for five or ten minutes. Then transfer to a wire rack, and cool completely. If you wish, frost with cream cheese or other frosting.

☞Cream Cheese Frosting☜

Cream cheese is the traditional frosting to go with carrot cake.

6 ounces (170 grams) cream cheese, softened

2 tablespoons (30 milliliters) honey or 1/4 cup (60 milliliters) sugar

1 teaspoon (5 milliliters) vanilla extract

1. Use a blender, food processor, or electric mixer. Blend together cream cheese, honey or sugar, and vanilla extract, until smooth.

2. Chill to make it firm enough for frosting and decorating.

Part Four

sources, Information & Support

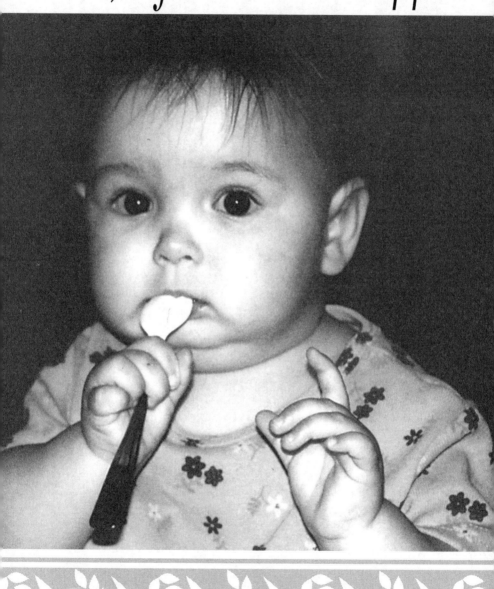

Books

ese are the best and most up-to-date of the books on feeding babies and chil-
en, and on breastfeeding, nutritional issues, and food safety.

American Academy of Pediatrics. *Pediatric Nutrition Handbook,* third edition, ed.
Dr. Lewis A. Barness. Elk Grove Village, IL: American Academic of Pediatrics,
1993.

Naomi Baumslag and Dia L. Michels. *Milk, Money, and Madness: The Culture and
Politics of Breastfeeding.* Westport, CT: Bergin & Garvey, 1995.

La Leche League International. THE WOMANLY ART OF BREASTFEEDING: Fortieth
Anniversary Edition. Schaumburg, IL, 1997.

Cheryl Mendelson. *Home Comforts: The Art and Science of Keeping House.* New York:
Scribner's, 1999.

Lucy Moll. *The Vegetarian Child: A Complete Guide for Parents.* New York:
Perigree, 1997.

Fred Pescatore. *Feed Your Kids Well: How to Help Your Child Lose Weight and Get
Healthy.* New York: Wiley, 1998.

Joseph C. Piscatella. *Fat-Proof Your Child.* New York: Workman, 1997.

Susan B. Roberts and Melvin B. Heyman, with Lisa Tracy. *Feeding Your Child for
Lifelong Health: Birth through Age Six.* New York: Bantam, 1999

William Sears and Martha Sears. T*he Family Nutrition Book: Everything You Need to
Know about Feeding Your Children—From Birth Through Adolescence.* Boston: Little,
Brown, 1999.

Carol Simontacchi. *The Crazy Makers: How the Food Industry Is Destroying Our Brains
and Harming Our Children.* New York: Tarcher/Putnam, 2000.

Dorothy D. Stallone and Michael F. Jacobson. *Cheating Babies: Nutritional Quality
and Cost of Commercial Baby Food.* Washington DC: Center for Science in the
Public Interest, 1995.

O. Robin Sweet and Thomas A. Bloom. *The Well Fed Baby.* New York:
Morrow, 2000.

Denise Webb. *Every Mother's Survival Guide To Feeding Infants and Young Children: with Nutrition Information on More Than 1,500 Brand-Name Products.* New York: Bantam, 1995.

Ruth Yaron. *Super Baby Food: Absolutely Everything You Should Know about Feeding Your Baby and Toddler from Starting Solid Foods to Age Three,* second edition. Archbald, PA: F. J. Roberts, 1998.

Websites

These are among the best websites on baby food, breastfeeding, and nutritional issues, up and running as of the year 2001. Also, see the websites associated with organizations.

www.aap.org

The American Academy of Pediatrics is "dedicated to the health, safety, and well-being of infants, children, adolescents, and young adults." The website features sales of books on cooking for children and children's nutrition.

www.babymilkaction.org

Baby Milk Action (UK) is the breastfeeding advocacy group located in Great Britain and associated with the World Health Organization.

www.ibfan.org

The International Baby Food Action Network (IBFAN) consists of more than 150 public interest groups working around the world in more than 90 countries. The goal is to reduce infant and young child morbidity and mortality, "to improve the health and well being of babies and young children, their mothers, and their families through the protection, promotion, and support of breastfeeding and optimal infant feeding practices."

www.fda.gov

This is the website for the United States Food and Drug Administration. You can also reach the FDA at 1-888-INFO-FDA

www.infactcanada.ca

The International Baby Food Action Coalition Canada (IBFACT), located in Toronto, is the North American representative of IBFAN, and "works to promote optimal infant and maternal health through the protection, promotion, and support of breastfeeding."

www.nabahomepage.org

The National Alliance for Breastfeeding Advocacy (NABA) "works to promote breastfeeding as a public health issue," and is linked to IBFAN.

www.veg.org.veg

The "Vegetarian Pages" provide a guide to Internet resources for vegetarian eating.

www.navigator.tufts.edu

The Tufts University "Nutrition Navigator" provides a guide to nutrition information on the Internet, although giant food corporations—including a commercial baby food company—sponsor some of their links.

ganizations

ese organizations offer excellent resources, information, advocacy, d support.

The Center for Science in the Public Interest
1875 Connecticut Avenue NW, Suite 300
Washington DC 20009 USA
202-332-9110

www.cspinet.org

CSPI is "a nonprofit education and advocacy organization that focuses on improving the safety and nutritional quality of our food supply..." and to ensure that advances in science are used for the public good. You may be interested in the CSPI Nutrition Action newsletter.

International Childbirth Education Association
P. O. Box 20048
Minneapolis MN 55420 USA
952-854-8660

www.icea.org

ICEA offers information and support on family-centered maternity and childbirth care.

International Lactation Consultant Association
1500 Sunday Drive, Suite 102
Raleigh NY 27607 USA
919-787-5181

www.ilca.org

ILCA provides referrals to lactation consultants and "promotes the professional development, advancement, and recognition of lactation consultants worldwide for the benefit of breastfeeding women, infants and children."

La Leche League International
1400 North Meacham Road
Schaumburg IL 60173-4840 USA
847-519-7730

www.lalecheleague.org

LLLI's mission "is to help mothers worldwide to breastfeed through mother-to-mother support, encouragement, information and education, and to promote a better understanding of breastfeeding as an important element in the healthy development of the baby and mother."

Nursing Mothers' Counsel
www.nursingmothers.org

This is a "non-affiliated, non-profit organization whose goal is to help mothers enjoy a relaxed and happy feeding relationship with their babies by providing breastfeeding information and support." Support includes 24-hour referral hot lines. National hot line is 650-599-3669.

Index
Whole Foods for Babies & Toddlers

⋙ A ⋘

⋙ B ⋘

➥ D ➥

➥ E ➥

➥ F ➥

❦ G ❦

❦ H ❦

⟿ I ⟿

⟿ J ⟿

⟿ K ⟿

⟿ L ⟿

⟿ M ⟿

≈ N ≈

≈ O ≈

〰️ P 〰️

〰️ Q 〰️

〰️ R 〰️

〰️ S 〰️

❧ **T** ❧

≈ U ≈

≈ V ≈

W

X

Y

Z

About La Leche League

La Leche League International offers many benefits to breastfeeding mothers and babies. Local La Leche League Groups meet monthly in communities all over the world, giving breastfeeding mothers the information they need and the opportunity to learn from one another. La Leche League Leaders, women who have nursed their own babies and who have met accreditation requirements, are only a phone call away. They provide accurate information on breastfeeding problems and can lend a sensitive ear to women with breastfeeding worries. You don't have to be a La Leche League member to contact a Leader or attend Group meetings. However, members receive added benefits. They receive LLLI's bimonthly magazine, NEW BEGINNINGS, which is filled with breastfeeding information, stories from nursing mothers, tips on discipline and common toddler problems, and news about breastfeeding from all over the world. Members also receive a 10% discount on purchases from LLLI's extensive Catalogue of carefully selected books, tapes, pamphlets, pumps, and other products for families. Members may also borrow books from local Group libraries. Membership is $30 a year in the USA and helps support the work of local LLL Groups as well as LLL projects all over the world. You can pay your dues to the LLL Group in your area or directly to LLLI.

For more information on a Group and Leaders near you, call 1-800-LA LECHE. (In Canada, call 1-800-665-4324 or 613-448-1842.) You can also visit our award winning website at www.lalecheleague.org for more information about LLLI and resources for breastfeeding support. In addition to finding information on membership or a Group near you, you can also find links to Group pages in the USA and all around the world. You can learn about the history of La Leche League International, browse the LLLI Catalogue, or peruse a collection of articles and selected passages from LLLI publications. The website also offers information and schedules for online LLL meetings as well as information on upcoming educational opportunities offered by LLLI.